A Note on the Editor of This Revised Edition

JAMES A. BEARD is one of this country's most eminent authorities on both food and drink. He is a consultant to a number of internationally known firms that produce or import the finest wines and spirits.

Among Mr. Beard's books that deal with drink as well as food are *Cook It Outdoors*, *The Fireside Cookbook*, *James Beard's Fish Cookery*, *Paris Cuisine*, and *How to Eat Better for Less Money*. His articles have appeared in *Harper's Bazaar*, *McCall's*, *House and Garden*, *Argosy*, and many journals of the food and restaurant industries. Mr. Beard believes in personally testing his recipes and recommendations. The kitchen in his New York apartment is a workshop where he spends most of his time while at home experimenting with good food and drink.

The Standard

BARTENDER'S GUIDE

BY

PATRICK GAVIN DUFFY

•

Revised and enlarged by

JAMES A. BEARD

PUBLISHED BY POCKET BOOKS, INC. NEW YORK

THE STANDARD BARTENDER'S GUIDE

Garden City edition published June, 1940

A *Pocket Book* edition

1st printing.........August, 1948
20th printing........March, 1965

The Vintage Chart on pages 208-220 is courtesy of *Gourmet*.

This *Pocket Book* edition, newly revised and enlarged especially for Pocket Books, Inc., has been printed from brand-new plates made from completely reset, clear, easy-to-read type. *Pocket Book* editions are published by Pocket Books, Inc., and are printed and distributed in the U.S.A. by Affiliated Publishers, a division of Pocket Books, Inc., 630 Fifth Avenue, New York, N.Y. 10020. Trademark of Pocket Books, Inc., 630 Fifth Avenue, New York, N.Y. 10020, registered in the United States and other countries.

L

Printed in the U.S.A.

TABLE OF CONTENTS

INTRODUCTION

The mixed drink, a wonderful American invention, steadily grows more popular in this country and elsewhere in the world. As with great culinary achievements, skill in mixing drinks comes with knowledge and practice. This book supplies the knowledge: over 1200 recipes for cocktails that have won public approval in the last hundred years. Practice comes naturally.

Whether he is a professional bartender or an amateur drink-mixer in his own home, the reader can judge for himself how extensive shall be his collection of spirits, wines, liqueurs and flavorings. I can only suggest that quantity is not a substitute for quality. No mixed drink is any better than its ingredients.

The book's author, Patrick Gavin Duffy, compiled his basic list of cocktails from the records of famous bars and restaurants in the United States, Canada, Europe and South America. He listed the makings of popular regional drinks and the formulas for festive punches served in great homes and hotel ballrooms. Mainly as a matter of historical completeness, he also set down the recipes for a number of mixed drinks that originated in the speakeasies of the Prohibition years, 1917-33. From these mixtures he withheld his personal endorsement, saying: "The majority . . . of cocktails are wholesome and well-concocted, but we cannot approve of those which include Gin, Scotch, Brandy, Vermouth and Cream in one drink."

With this sentiment I heartily agree. The ideal cocktail is a blend, not a conflict of flavors. Strange mixtures were common in speakeasies, partly because bartenders were forced to conceal the poor quality of their liquors. But since no one today would want to taste them, the curiosities of the Volstead Era have been omitted from this revised edition.

Among other changes in this edition are recipes for new or rediscovered drinks and altered directions for several classic cocktails. Like all else, tastes change with the times. Witness the current trend toward dryness in apéritifs; the immense popularity of the very dry Martini and the dry Old-Fashioned. When the last edition of the *Guide* was published, the Gibson was a not-so-dry Martini containing a cherry. Today that would be unthinkable.

Even with timely changes, omissions and additions, the reader of average taste will find that the *Guide* contains many odd or unfamiliar drinks. These drinks exist. Some are good; some are excellent. And because this book is intended for the professional bartender as well as the amateur, it must contain mixtures for which there is only an occasional demand. So don't look askance at the "Widow's Kiss" or "Polly's Special" or other such rarities. Somewhere, with some people, they are favorites.

The wine section in this edition has been revised as an up-to-date commentary on serving and drinking the best American and European wines, and it includes a new wine chart for the years 1945-57. This chart was prepared by the eminent wine authority Frank Schoonmaker, especially for Sherry Wine and Spirits Company, Inc., of New York, and is republished here by courtesy of Sam Aaron, president.

Another useful addition to the *Guide* is a chapter suggesting what foods to serve with cocktails in both home and restaurant. Still other innovations are a glossary defining all principal spirits, wines, liqueurs and flavorings used in mixing drinks, and a summary of standard bar measurements.

—*James A. Beard*

The Standard

BARTENDER'S GUIDE

GLOSSARY

Abricotine: One of the many French apricot liqueurs.

Ale: A malt brew (see BEER) darker and bitterer than beer. Alcoholic content about 6%.

Amer Picon: A French apéritif wine, flavored with aromatics. Rather sweet.

Angostura Bitters: See BITTERS.

Anisette: A colorless liqueur with an anise flavor.

Apéritif: A drink of moderate alcoholic content, taken before meals, ostensibly to give one an appetite.

Applejack: The common name for apple brandy. Sometimes applies to the home-made product.

Arrack: An Oriental drink of high alcoholic content, generally made from rice. Called the original spirit.

Bacardi: A brand of Cuban or Puerto Rican rum.

Beer: A liquor, generally light-colored, fermented from cereals and malt, flavored with hops. Alcoholic strength about 4%.

Benedictine: One of the oldest of the herb-flavored liqueurs. A Benedictine monk created the recipe which has remained a secret.

Bitters: An infusion of aromatics for flavoring cocktails and other drinks. Angostura, Fernet Branca and Peychaud's are among those most frequently used.

Bottled in Bond: A term meaning that the distiller agreed under law to store his whiskey in bonded warehouses without paying the excise tax until he was ready to withdraw the whiskey from the warehouses. The law provides that whiskey so bottled and stored must be at least four years old and 100 proof. The stamp "Bottled in Bond" is not a guarantee of quality.

Bourbon: A whiskey distilled from mash not less than 51% of which was corn grain.

Brandy: A liquor made by the distillation of wine or a fermented fruit mash. When the term *brandy* is used without other qualification it refers to that which is made from grape wine. Cognac refers to brandy distilled in the region around the city of Cognac in France. Armagnac comes from the section around Condom. The white alcohols are called brandies as well.

Byrrh: A reddish French apéritif wine, flavored with aromatics.

Calisay: A Spanish liqueur with a bitterish after-taste.

Calvados: A French apple brandy distilled in Normandy.

Chartreuse: This liqueur comes in two colors and two strengths. Yellow chartreuse is lighter and the green is heavier. Both are made from a wide variety of herbs and aromatics and were originated by a French order of monks.

Cognac: See BRANDY.

Cointreau: A colorless sweet liqueur with an orange flavor.

Crème de Cacao: A dark brown liqueur made of cocoa beans, spices and vanilla with a brandy base.

Crème de Cassis: A dark red liqueur, or syrup, made from black currants.

Crème de Menthe: A peppermint-flavored liqueur which comes in three colors: white, green or red.

Crème de Rose: A liqueur flavored with rose petals.

Crème de Vanille: A liqueur flavored with vanilla.

Crème de Violette: A lavender-colored liqueur, made from vanilla and cacao with a violet bouquet.

Crème d'Yvette: A liqueur similar to Crème de Violette but with a pronounced violet taste.

Curaçao: A liqueur made from the peel of Curaçao oranges which are grown on the West Indian Island of Curaçao.

Dubonnet: A French apéritif wine made from aromatics. It has a slight quinine taste.

Fernet Branca: See BITTERS.

Fraise: A brandy made from strawberries.

Framboise: A brandy made from raspberries.

Gin: A liquor made with a neutral spirit base and flavored, generally, with juniper berries. Old Tom Gin is a sweet gin. Holland Gin, because of its heavy body and distinctive flavor, is usually drunk straight. Most American and British gins are similar, save for individual brand flavorings.

Grand Marnier: A reddish liqueur with an orange flavor and Cognac base. Somewhat similar to Curaçao.

Grenadine: A red, artificially flavored syrup for sweetening.

Kirsch: A colorless brandy distilled from a small black cherry.

Kümmel: A colorless liqueur with a caraway flavor.

Liqueurs: These alcoholic drinks are usually made by adding an infusion of fruits or herbs to grain alcohol, brandy, Cognac or whiskey. They are generally served after meals because of their sweetness, but are also frequently used as flavoring in cocktails or punches.

Maraschino: A strong sweet liqueur with a pronounced bittersweet cherry taste.

Noyau: A liqueur made with a brandy base flavored with a variety of fruits and bitter almond.

Orange Bitters: A flavoring with a bittersweet orange taste used in cocktails and other drinks.

Orgeat: A flavoring syrup with a bittersweet almond taste.

Pernod: The present-day substitute for absinthe, which has been banned because of the wormwood used in its manufacture. Pernod is used as an apéritif and as an ingredient in many cocktails.

Proof: The measurement of alcoholic strength. Each degree of proof equals 1/2 of 1% of alcohol. Thus 100 proof equals 50% alcohol.

Prunelle: A liqueur with the fragrance and flavor of plum.

Quinquina: A reddish brown aromatic wine, flavored with quinine and herbs. The word is often used in referring to other apéritif wines.

Rum: A liquor made from the fermentation and distillation of sugar cane. The color of rum has nothing to do with its alcoholic content but the flavor of the darker rums is stronger than that of the light varieties, the result of additional flavoring matter and caramel.

Rye: A whiskey distilled from mash not less than 51% of which was rye grain.

Scotch Whisky: A product of Scotland distilled from a mash of grain, primarily barley.

Sloe Gin: A liqueur made of gin and sloe berries.

Southern Comfort: An American liqueur with a bourbon base and a peach flavor.

Swedish Punch: A pale yellowish liqueur with a slight rum flavor.

Tequila: A Mexican alcoholic drink distilled from pulque.

Triple Sec: A colorless liqueur with a sweet orange flavor.

Vermouth, Dry: A dry, aromatic apéritif wine, most frequently used in this country as an ingredient for cocktails.

Vermouth, Sweet: An aromatic apéritif wine, sweet and more highly flavored than the dry. Used mainly in cocktails.

Vodka: The Russian national drink. It is also made in this country and is rapidly gaining popularity. It is colorless and nearly tasteless and can be used in almost any drink calling for gin.

Whiskey: The general name for liquors of not less than 80 proof distilled from a mash of grain. Only Scotch whisky is spelled without the *e*.

STANDARD BAR MEASUREMENTS

1 quart	32 ounces
1 pint	16 ounces
4/5 quart (fifth)	25.6 ounces
1 wineglass (average)	4 ounces
1 jigger	1 1/2 ounces
1 pony	1 ounce
1 teaspoon	1/8 ounce (approx.)
2 teaspoons	1 dessertspoon
3 teaspoons	1 tablespoon
1 cup	8 ounces
1 dash	1/32 ounce (approx.)
1/2 bottle wine	12 ounces
1 bottle wine (average)	24 ounces
split of Champagne	6 1/2 ounces
quart of Champagne	26 ounces
Magnum (two bottles)	52 ounces
Jeroboam (four bottles)	104 ounces
Rehoboam (six bottles)	156 ounces (1 gallon, 1 pint, 12 ounces)

CHAMPAGNE

Because of the nature of this very special wine, all drinks using it as a base, regardless of their type, have been placed together in this section.

Alfonso Cocktail

1/2 Jigger Dubonnet
1 Cube Ice
1 Dash Bitters
1 Lump Sugar

Place the Sugar in a large saucer Champagne glass and sprinkle with Bitters. Add Ice and Dubonnet and fill with iced Champagne. Serve with twist of Lemon Peel.

Barbotage of Champagne

Fill a tumbler 1/2 full of finely cracked ice. Add 1 dash of Angostura Bitters, 1 teaspoon each of Sugar Syrup and Lemon Juice, and fill with iced Champagne. Stir lightly and serve with twist of Orange Peel.

Blue Train Cocktail No. 2

Shake well together with cracked ice, 1/4 Brandy and 1/4 lightly sweetened Pineapple Juice. Fill glass 1/2 full with this mixture and fill with iced Champagne.

Champagne Cobbler

Fill a large goblet 2/3 full of cracked ice. Add 1/2 teaspoon Lemon Juice and 1/2 teaspoon Curaçao. Stir and add

1 thin slice of Orange and 1 small Pineapple stick. Fill with iced Champagne. Stir lightly again and serve with a straw.

Champagne Cocktail No. 1

Place 1 small lump Sugar in a Champagne glass and sprinkle with 1 small dash Angostura Bitters. Add 1 small twist each Orange and Lemon Peel. Fill with iced Champagne. Muddle gently.

Champagne Cocktail No. 2

Place 2/3 jigger Southern Comfort, 1 dash Angostura Bitters and 1 twist of Lemon Peel in a large saucer Champagne glass. Fill with iced Champagne.

Champagne Cooler

Place in a tall glass, 1/2 filled with ice, 2/3 jigger Brandy, 2/3 jigger Cointreau and fill up with chilled Champagne. Stir and garnish with Mint.

Champagne Cup No. 1 (for 12 to 16)

Place in a punch bowl, with a block of ice, 1/2 Pineapple cut in slices, 6 good slivers of Cucumber rind, 1 box of fresh Strawberries, 3 jiggers Curaçao, 1 quart Soda Water, and stir lightly. Add 2 bottles iced Champagne. Stir lightly again and serve.

Champagne Cup No. 2 (for 10 or 12)

Place in a punch bowl, with a block of ice, 2 tablespoons Powdered Sugar, 2 jiggers Cognac, 1/2 jigger Curaçao, 1/4 jigger Maraschino, 1/4 jigger Grand Marnier and 1 Orange, sliced thin and seeded. Add 1 or 2 quarts iced Champagne and decorate with Pineapple, Maraschino Cherries and fresh Mint.

Champagne Fizz

Place the juice of 1 Orange in a highball glass with several ice cubes. Fill with iced Champagne.

Champagne Julep

Crush 4 sprigs Mint with 1 lump of Sugar and a few drops of water in bottom of your tallest highball glass. Half fill with cracked ice and add 1 jigger Brandy. Fill with Champagne and decorate with extra Mint. Serve with straws.

Champagne Punch No. 1 (1 gallon)

Combine in punch bowl 1/2 pound Powdered Sugar, 1 quart Soda Water, 2 jiggers Brandy, 2 jiggers Maraschino, 2 jiggers Curaçao, 3 jiggers Lemon Juice. Stir together and add block of ice. Pour in 2 or 3 bottles Champagne. Decorate as desired.

Champagne Punch No. 2 (for 18)

Combine in the order named in a large punch bowl, with a block of ice, juice of 2 Oranges, juice of 2 Lemons, 1/2 cup Sugar, 1/2 cup Light Rum, 1/2 Dark Rum, 1 cup Pineapple Juice. Stir lightly and pour in 2 bottles iced Champagne. Serve in punch glasses, decorated with fruit as desired.

Champagne Punch No. 3 (for 20)

Place 1 quart either Lemon or Orange Ice in a punch bowl. Pour over it 2–3 bottles iced Champagne.

Champagne Punch No. 4 (for 15)

Place large block of ice in punch bowl. Add 2 jiggers Brandy, 2 jiggers Cointreau and 2 bottles iced Champagne.

Champagne Punch No. 5 (for 10)

Combine in punch bowl, with lots of ice, 1 jigger Maraschino, 1 jigger Yellow Chartreuse, 2 jiggers Brandy, 1 pint Soda Water, 2 teaspoons Sugar and 1 bottle iced Champagne.

Champagne Punch No. 6 (for 12)

Combine in punch bowl 1 jigger Brandy, 1 jigger Curaçao, 1 jigger Maraschino, 2 sliced seeded Lemons, 2 sliced seeded Oranges and 1/2 basket Strawberries or Raspberries. Add 1 bottle iced Soda Water and 2 bottles iced Champagne, or omit the Soda Water and add 3 bottles iced Champagne. Place the punch bowl to chill in a bed of shaved ice and serve.

Champagne Punch No. 7 (Dragoon Punch) (for 20)

This Punch is reputedly the cavalry man's answer to ARTILLERY PUNCH (see Index). Blend in a large punch bowl 3 pints Porter, 3 pints Ale, 1/2 pint Brandy, 1/2 pint Sherry, 1/2 pint Sugar Syrup and 3 Lemons, sliced thin. Immediately before serving, add a block of ice and 2 bottles iced Champagne.

Champagne Punch No. 8 (individual)

Fill a large tumbler or highball glass 1/2 full of ice. Add the juice of 1/2 Lemon, 1/2 jigger Framboise, 1 slice of Orange and fill with iced Champagne. Stir lightly and serve with straws.

Champagne Velvet (Black Velvet)

Half fill a tall glass with iced Stout. Fill with iced Champagne as desired. Pour very slowly or glass will overflow.

French "75"

1 Jigger Dry Gin
1/3 Jigger Lemon Juice
1 Teaspoon Powdered Sugar

Pour into tall glass 1/2 full of cracked ice, and fill with chilled Champagne.

French "95"

Prepare same as FRENCH "75," using Bourbon Whiskey instead of Gin.

French "125"

Prepare same as FRENCH "75," using Brandy for Gin.

Friendly Sons of St. Patrick Shandy Gaff (see Champagne Velvet)

I. B. F. Pick-Me-Up Cocktail

1 Jigger Brandy
3 Dashes Curaçao
3 Dashes Fernet Branca
1 Cube Ice

Place in large saucer Champagne glass and fill with iced Champagne. Squeeze Lemon Peel over top.

King's Peg

Place a piece of ice in a large wine glass. Pour in 1 jigger Brandy and fill with iced Champagne.

London Special

Place in a large highball glass 1 lump Sugar, a large twist Orange Peel, 1 cube of ice, and 2 dashes Peychaud's Bitters. Muddle well and fill with iced Champagne.

Mimosa

Place a cube of ice in large wine glass. Add the juice of 1/2 Orange. Fill with iced Champagne and stir.

Peach Bowl No. 1

Place in a large goblet 1 washed unpeeled perfect Peach. Cover with iced Champagne. Prick the Peach several times to release the flavor and serve. The Peach, incidentally, is delicious eating after the drink is finished.

Peach Bowl No. 2

This is prepared same as PEACH BOWL No. 1, but with a Brandied Peach and a little of the Syrup. And you don't need to prick the Peach to get the flavor!

Prince of Wales

Place in a shaker 1 dash Angostura Bitters, 1 teaspoon Curaçao, and 1/2 jigger each Madeira and Brandy. Shake well with ice and strain into a large wine glass. Fill with iced Champagne and serve with a thin slice of Orange.

Queen's Peg

Place a cube of ice in a large wine glass. Add 1/2 jigger Dry Gin and fill with iced Champagne.

Soyer-au-Champagne Cocktail

Place in a large saucer Champagne glass 1 large teaspoon Vanilla Ice Cream, 2 dashes Maraschino, 2 dashes Curaçao, 2 dashes Brandy and stir together gently. Fill with iced Champagne and decorate with a slice of Orange and a Cherry.

BASIC COBBLER

The Cobbler, which like the Julep is a drink of American origin, is generally served in a large goblet. Fill 2/3 full of shaved or finely cracked ice. Sprinkle with 1 teaspoon fine granulated Sugar, if desired, and pour in 1 or 2 jiggers Claret, Port, Rhine Wine, Sauterne or Sherry; or, if preferred, 1 or 2 jiggers Applejack, Brandy, Gin, Rum, Whiskey or Vodka. Whatever is used the glass should be decorated with a slice of Orange and a small Pineapple stick. Frequently Mint is used.

SPECIAL COBBLERS

Brandy Cobbler

Fill a tumbler 3/4 full of cracked ice. Add 1 teaspoon Curaçao, 1/2 teaspoon Sugar, 1 or 2 jiggers Brandy. Decorate with fruit and serve.

Champagne Cobbler (see Champagne)

Claret Cobbler

Fill a tumbler 1/2 full of cracked ice. Add 1 dash Maraschino, 1 teaspoon each Sugar and Lemon Juice. Fill with Claret and stir. Decorate with fruit and serve.

Port Cobbler

Fill a tumbler 2/3 full of cracked ice. Add 1 teaspoon each Orange Juice and Curaçao. Fill with Port Wine. Decorate with fruit and serve. A very little Sugar may be added if desired.

Rhine Wine Cobbler

Fill a tumbler 1/2 full of cracked ice. Add 1 teaspoon each Sugar and Lemon Juice. Stir lightly and fill with Rhine Wine. Decorate with twist of Lemon Peel and Mint.

Sauterne Cobbler

Prepare same as RHINE WINE COBBLER, omitting Sugar and Mint.

Sherry Cobbler

Fill a tumbler 2/3 full of cracked ice. Add a teaspoon each Sugar and Orange Juice. Fill with Sherry, stir slightly, decorate with fruit and serve.

COCKTAILS

APÉRITIF AND WINE BASES

AMER PICON

Picon

1/2 Amer Picon
1/2 Dry Vermouth

Stir well with ice and strain into glass.

Picon Grenadine

1 Jigger Amer Picon
1/2 Jigger Grenadine

Place with ice cubes in Old-Fashioned glass and fill with Soda Water.

BYRRH

Byrrh

1/3 Byrrh
1/3 Rye Whiskey
1/3 Dry Vermouth

Stir well with ice and strain into glass.

Byrrh Cassis

2/3 Byrrh
1/3 Crème de Cassis

Place in glass with ice cubes and fill with Soda Water.

Byrrh Special

1/2 Byrrh
1/2 Old Tom Gin

Stir well with ice and strain into glass.

CALISAY

Calisay

1/2 Calisay
1/2 Sweet Vermouth
3 Dashes Sugar Syrup

Stir well with ice and strain into glass.

Montauk Riding Club

1 Jigger Calisay
1 Jigger Brandy
3 Dashes Lime Juice
2 Dashes Sugar Syrup

Shake well with ice and strain into glass.

DUBONNET

Appetizer No. 1

1 Jigger Dubonnet
Juice of 1/2 Orange

Shake well with ice and strain into glass.

Bob Danby

1 Jigger Dubonnet
1/2 Jigger Brandy

Stir well with ice and strain into glass.

Dubonnet Manhattan

1/2 Dubonnet
1/2 Whiskey

Stir well with ice and serve with Cherry.

Mary Garden

1/2 Dubonnet
1/2 Dry Vermouth

Stir well with ice and strain into glass. When served with a twist of Lemon Peel, this is called a MERRY WIDOW.

On-the-Rocks

Place twist of Lemon Peel and ice in Old-Fashioned glass. Then fill with Dubonnet.

Sanctuary

1/2 Dubonnet
1/4 Amer Picon
1/4 Cointreau

Stir well with ice and strain into glass.

Upstairs

2 Jiggers Dubonnet
Juice of 1/4 Lemon

Pour into large cocktail glass with ice cubes and fill with Soda Water.

Weep No More

1/3 Dubonnet
1/3 Brandy
1/3 Lime Juice
1 Dash Maraschino

Stir well with ice and strain into glass.

FERNET BRANCA

Yodel

1/2 Fernet Branca
1/2 Orange Juice

Place ice cube in glass and combine ingredients. Fill with Soda Water.

LILLET

Roy Howard

1/2 Lillet
1/4 Brandy
1/4 Orange Juice
2 Dashes Grenadine

Shake well with ice and strain into glass.

PERNOD

All drinks that call for Absinthe may be made with Pernod.

Brunelle

1/4 Pernod
3/4 Lemon Juice
1-1/2 Teaspoons Sugar

Shake well with ice and strain into glass.

Button Hook

1/4 Pernod
1/4 Apricot Brandy
1/4 Brandy
1/4 White Crème de Menthe

Shake well with ice and strain into glass.

Duchess

1/3 Pernod
1/3 Dry Vermouth
1/3 Sweet Vermouth

Shake well with ice and strain into glass.

Frappé (with Pernod)

1 Jigger Pernod
1/3 Jigger Anisette
2 Dashes Angostura Bitters

Shake well with shaved ice and strain into glass.

Glad Eye

2/3 Pernod
1/3 Peppermint

Shake well with ice and strain into glass.

Macaroni

2/3 Pernod
1/3 Sweet Vermouth

Shake well with ice and strain into glass.

Nine-Pick

1/3 Pernod
1/3 Curaçao
1/3 Brandy
1 Egg Yolk

Shake well with ice and strain into glass.

Nineteen-Pick-Me-Up

2/3 Pernod
1/3 Gin
1 Dash Angostura Bitters
1 Dash Orange Bitters
1 Dash Sugar Syrup

Shake well with ice and strain into glass. Add dash of Soda Water.

Pansy

1 Jigger Pernod
6 Dashes Grenadine
2 Dashes Angostura Bitters

Shake well with ice and strain into glass.

Pernod No. 1

3/4 Pernod
1/4 Water
1 Dash Sugar Syrup
1 Dash Angostura Bitters

Shake well with ice and strain into glass.

Pernod No. 2

Prepare same as No. 1, using Pernod and Water half and half.

Suisse

1 Jigger Pernod
4 Dashes Anisette
1 Egg White

Shake well with ice and strain into glass. Sugar Syrup may be used in place of Anisette.

Victory

1/2 Pernod
1/2 Grenadine

Shake well with ice and strain into glass. Fill with Soda Water.

Which Way **(see White Way No. 2 on page 94)**

PORT

Broken Spur

2/3 White Port
1/6 Dry Gin
1/6 Sweet Vermouth
1 Egg Yolk
1 Teaspoon Anisette

Shake well with ice and strain into glass.

Chocolate No. 1

3/4 Port
1/4 Yellow Chartreuse
1 Egg Yolk
1 Teaspoon Crushed Chocolate

Shake well with ice and strain into glass.

Devil's

1/2 Port
1/2 Dry Vermouth
2 Dashes Lemon Juice

Stir well with ice and strain into glass.

Port No. 1

2 Jiggers Port
1 Dash Brandy

Stir well with ice and strain into glass. Squeeze Orange Peel over top.

Port No. 2

2 Jiggers Port
2 Dashes Curaçao
1 Dash Orange Bitters
1 Dash Angostura Bitters

Stir well with ice and strain into glass.

Port Sangaree

2 Jiggers Port
1 Jigger Water
1/2 Teaspoon Powdered Sugar

Stir well with ice and strain into glass.

PUNCH BASE

After-Dinner Special

1 Jigger Swedish Punch
1/2 Jigger Cherry Brandy
Juice of 1/2 Lime

Shake well with ice and strain into glass.

Bombay No. 1

2 Jiggers East Indian Punch
4 Dashes Lemon Juice

Stir well with ice and strain into glass.

Doctor

1 Jigger Swedish Punch
Juice of 1 Lime

Stir well with ice and strain into glass.

East and West

3/4 East Indian Punch
1/4 Light Rum
1 Dash Lemon Juice

Stir well with ice and strain into glass.

Grand Slam

1/2 Swedish Punch
1/4 Sweet Vermouth
1/4 Dry Vermouth

Stir well with ice and strain into glass.

Hesitation

3/4 Swedish Punch
1/4 Rye Whiskey
1 Dash Lemon Juice

Stir well with ice and strain into glass.

Hundred Per Cent

2/3 Swedish Punch
1/6 Lemon Juice
1/6 Orange Juice
2 Dashes Grenadine

Stir well with ice and strain into glass.

Margaret Duffy

2/3 Swedish Punch
1/3 Brandy
2 Dashes Bitters

Stir well with ice and strain into glass.

Waldorf No. 1

1/2 Swedish Punch
1/4 Dry Gin
1/4 Lemon or Lime Juice

Stir well with ice and strain into glass.

SHERRY

Adonis

2/3 Dry Sherry
1/3 Sweet Vermouth
1 Dash Orange Bitters

Stir well with ice and strain into glass.

Bamboo

1/2 Sherry
1/2 Sweet Vermouth
1 Dash Angostura Bitters

Stir well with ice and strain into glass.

Bomb (for 6)

6 Jiggers Sherry
1 Jigger Cointreau
1 Jigger Orange Juice
1 Dash Orange Bitters
2 Dashes Pimento Dram

Shake well with shaved ice and serve with an Olive.

Brazil

1/2 Sherry
1/2 Dry Vermouth
1 Dash Pernod
1 Dash Angostura Bitters

Stir well with ice and strain into glass. Squeeze Lemon Peel over top.

Byculla

1/4 Sherry
1/4 Port
1/4 Curaçao
1/4 Ginger

Stir well with ice and strain into glass.

Coronation No. 1

1/2 Sherry
1/2 Dry Vermouth
1 Dash Maraschino
2 Dashes Orange Bitters

Stir well with ice and strain into glass.

Cupid

2 Jiggers Sherry
1 Egg
1 Teaspoon Powdered Sugar
1 Pinch Cayenne Pepper

Shake well with ice and strain into glass.

Duke of Marlborough

1/2 Sherry
1/2 Sweet Vermouth
3 Dashes Raspberry Syrup
Juice of 1 Lime

Shake well with ice and strain into glass.

East Indian

1/2 Sherry
1/2 Dry Vermouth
1 Dash Orange Bitters

Stir well with ice and strain into glass.

Greenbriar

2/3 Sherry
1/3 Dry Vermouth
1 Dash Peach Bitters
1 Sprig Fresh Mint

Shake well with ice and strain into glass.

Philomel

1/3 Sherry
1/6 Rum
1/4 Quinquina
1/4 Orange Juice
1 Pinch Pepper

Shake well with ice and strain into glass.

Pineapple (for 6)

Soak 1 cup crushed Pineapple in 4 jiggers Dry White Wine for 2 hours. Add 2 jiggers fresh Pineapple Juice, the juice of 1/4 Lemon and 6 jiggers Sherry. Chill the shaker thoroughly but do not put any ice in the mixture. Stir when cold and strain into glasses. Serve with a small wedge of Pineapple in each.

Plain Sherry

2 Jiggers Sherry
2 Dashes Maraschino
2 Dashes Pernod

Shake well with ice and strain into glass.

Reform

2/3 Sherry
1/3 Dry Vermouth
1 Dash Orange Bitters

Stir well with ice and strain into glass. Serve with a Cherry.

Sherry

2 Jiggers Sherry
4 Dashes Dry Vermouth
4 Dashes Orange Bitters

Stir well with ice and strain into glass.

Sherry and Egg

Carefully break 1 Egg into a cocktail glass, leaving the yolk intact. Fill the glass with Sherry.

Sherry Twist No. 1 (for 6)

6 Jiggers Sherry
2 Jiggers Dry Vermouth
2 Jiggers Brandy
1-1/2 Jiggers Cointreau
1/2 Jigger Lemon Juice
1 Small Piece of Cinnamon

Shake well with ice and strain into glasses.

Sherry Twist No. 2 (for 6)

5 Jiggers Sherry
4 Jiggers Whiskey
1 Jigger Cointreau
Juice of 1 Orange
Juice of 1/4 Lemon
2 Cloves
1 Pinch Cayenne Pepper

Shake well with ice and strain into glasses.

Ship

1/2 Sherry
1/8 Whiskey
2 Dashes Rum
2 Dashes Prune Syrup
2 Dashes Orange Bitters

Shake well with ice and strain into glass. A little Sugar may be added if desired.

Straight Law

2/3 Dry Sherry
1/3 Dry Gin

Stir well with ice and strain into glass. A twist of Lemon Peel may be added.

Tuxedo

2 Jiggers Sherry
1/2 Jigger Anisette
2 Dashes Maraschino
1 Dash Peychaud's Bitters

Stir well with ice and strain into glass.

Xeres

2 Jiggers Sherry
1 Dash Peach Bitters
1 Dash Orange Bitters

Stir well with ice and strain into glass.

VERMOUTH

Addington

1/2 Sweet Vermouth
1/2 Dry Vermouth

Stir well with ice and strain into large cocktail glass. Fill with Soda Water and serve with twist of Lemon Peel.

Alice Mine

1/4 Dry Vermouth
4 Dashes Sweet Vermouth
1/2 Grand Marnier
1/4 Dry Gin
1 Dash Angostura Bitters

Stir well with ice and strain into glass.

Bonsoni

2/3 Sweet Vermouth
1/3 Fernet Branca

Stir well with ice and strain into glass.

Cherry Mixture

1/2 Sweet Vermouth
1/2 Dry Vermouth
1 Dash Maraschino
1 Dash Angostura Bitters

Stir well with ice and strain into glass. Serve with a Cherry.

Chrysanthemum

1/2 Dry Vermouth
1/2 Benedictine
3 Dashes Pernod

Stir well with ice and strain into glass. Serve with twist of Orange Peel.

Cinzano

2 Jiggers Cinzano Vermouth
2 Dashes Orange Bitters
2 Dashes Angostura Bitters

Stir well with ice and strain into glass. Squeeze Orange Peel over top.

Crystal Bronx

1/2 Dry Vermouth
1/2 Sweet Vermouth
Juice of 1/4 Orange

Pour into large cocktail glass with ice and fill with Soda Water.

Diplomat

2/3 Dry Vermouth
1/3 Sweet Vermouth
1 Dash Maraschino

Stir well with ice and strain into glass. Add Cherry and squeeze Lemon Peel over top.

Fig Leaf

1 Jigger Sweet Vermouth
2/3 Jigger Light Rum
Juice of 1/2 Lime
1 Dash Angostura Bitters

Shake well with ice and strain into glass.

Green Room

2/3 Dry Vermouth
1/3 Brandy
2 Dashes Curaçao

Stir well with ice and strain.

Harvard Wine

2/3 Jigger Dry Vermouth
1/2 Jigger Brandy
1 Dash Orange Bitters

Stir well with ice and strain into large cocktail glass and fill up with Soda Water.

Humpty Dumpty

2/3 Dry Vermouth
1/3 Maraschino

Stir well with ice and strain into glass.

Italian

2/3 Sweet Vermouth
1/3 Fernet Branca
2 Dashes Sugar Syrup
1 Dash Pernod

Stir well with ice and strain into glass.

Nineteen

2/3 Dry Vermouth
1/6 Dry Gin
1/6 Kirsch
1 Dash Pernod
4 Dashes Sugar Syrup

Stir well with ice and strain into glass.

Pantomime

1 Jigger Dry Vermouth
1 Egg White
1 Dash Grenadine
1 Dash Orgeat Syrup

Shake well with ice and strain into glass.

Perfect

1 Jigger Dry Vermouth
1 Jigger Sweet Vermouth
1 Jigger Dry Gin

Stir well with ice and strain into glass. Serve with twist of Lemon Peel.

Perpetual

1/2 Sweet Vermouth
1/2 Dry Vermouth
4 Dashes Crème d'Yvette
2 Dashes Crème de Cacao

Stir well with ice and strain into glass.

Plain Vermouth (for 6)

10 Jiggers Dry Vermouth
1 Teaspoon Pernod
1 Teaspoon Maraschino

Stir well with ice and strain into glasses. Serve with a Cherry in each.

Queen Elizabeth Wine

2/3 Jigger Dry Vermouth
1/3 Jigger Benedictine
1/3 Lime or Lemon Juice

Stir well with ice and strain into glass.

Raymond Hitchcocktail

2 Jiggers Sweet Vermouth
1 Slice Pineapple
Juice of 1/2 Orange
1 Dash Orange Bitters

Stir well with ice and strain into glass.

Soul Kiss No. 1

1/3 Dry Vermouth
1/3 Sweet Vermouth
1/6 Dubonnet
1/6 Orange Juice

Stir well with ice and strain into glass.

Spion Kop

1/2 Dry Vermouth
1/2 Dubonnet

Stir well with ice and strain into glass.

Third Rail No. 1

1 Jigger Dry Vermouth
1 Dash Curaçao
1 Dash Mint

Stir well with ice and strain into glass. Serve with twist of Lemon Peel.

Trocadero

1/2 Dry Vermouth
1/2 Sweet Vermouth
1 Dash Grenadine
1 Dash Orange Bitters

Stir well with ice and strain into glass. Add Cherry and squeeze Lemon Peel over top.

Tropical

1/3 Dry Vermouth
1/3 Maraschino
1/3 Crème de Cacao
1 Dash Orange Bitters
1 Dash Angostura Bitters

Stir well with ice and strain into glass.

Vermouth Apéritif

Place cracked ice in a cocktail glass. Fill with Sweet Vermouth and serve with twist of Lemon Peel.

Vermouth No. 1

2 Jiggers Vermouth, Dry or Sweet
2 Dashes Angostura Bitters

Stir well with ice and strain into glass.

Vermouth No. 2

1-1/2 Jiggers Sweet Vermouth
1/2 Teaspoon Curaçao
1 Teaspoon Amer Picon
1/2 Teaspoon Powdered Sugar
1 Dash Angostura Bitters

Stir well with ice and strain into glass. Serve with twist of Lemon Peel and a Cherry.

Vermouth Cassis

2 Jiggers Dry Vermouth
2/3 Jigger Crème de Cassis

Place in glass with ice cubes and fill with Soda Water.

Vermouth Frappé

1-1/2 Jiggers Sweet Vermouth
1 Dash Angostura Bitters

Stir with shaved ice and strain into glass.

Vermouth Half and Half (see Addington on page 17)

Vermouth-on-the-Rocks

Fill Old-Fashioned glass with ice. Pour in Sweet Vermouth and serve with twist of Lemon Peel.

Washington

2/3 Dry Vermouth
1/3 Brandy
2 Dashes Sugar Syrup
2 Dashes Angostura Bitters

Stir well with ice and strain into glass.

Wyoming Swing

1/2 Sweet Vermouth
1/2 Dry Vermouth
1 Teaspoon Powdered Sugar
Juice of 1/4 Orange

Shake well with ice and strain into glass.

York Special

3/4 Dry Vermouth
1/4 Maraschino
4 Dashes Orange Bitters

Stir well with ice and strain into glass.

BRANDY AND COGNAC BASES

Alexander No. 1

1/3 Brandy
1/3 Crème de Cacao
1/3 Cream

Shake well with ice and strain into glass.

American Beauty

1/3 Brandy
1/3 Dry Vermouth
1/3 Orange Juice
1 Dash White Crème de Menthe
1 Dash Grenadine

Shake well with ice and strain into glass. Top carefully with a little Port.

Aunt Jemima

1/3 Brandy
1/3 Crème de Cacao
1/3 Benedictine

Pour ingredients carefully into a liqueur glass so that they are in separate layers. Serve after dinner.

B. and B.

1/2 Brandy
1/2 Benedictine

Serve in a liqueur glass or iced in a cocktail glass. This is an after-dinner drink.

Baltimore Bracer

1/2 Brandy
1/2 Anisette
1 Egg White

Shake well with ice and strain into glass.

Barney Barnato

1/2 Brandy
1/2 Dubonnet
1 Dash Angostura Bitters
1 Dash Curaçao

Stir well with ice and strain into glass.

Betsy Ross

1 Jigger Brandy
1 Jigger Port

2 Dashes Angostura Bitters
1 Dash Curaçao

Stir well with ice and strain into a large cocktail glass. As an eye-opener this may be made with the yolk of 1 Egg and 1 teaspoon of Sugar. Shake with ice and strain into glass and serve with a grating of Nutmeg.

Between-the-Sheets

1/3 Brandy
1/3 Cointreau
1/3 Light Rum

Shake well with ice and strain into glass.

Big Boy

1/2 Brandy
1/4 Cointreau
1/4 Sirop de Citron

Stir well with ice and strain into glass.

Block and Fall

1/3 Brandy
1/3 Cointreau
1/6 Calvados or Apple Brandy
1/6 Pernod

Shake well with ice and strain into glass.

Bombay

1/2 Brandy
1/4 Sweet Vermouth
1/4 Dry Vermouth
2 Dashes Curaçao
1 Dash Pernod

Stir well with ice and strain into glass.

Booster

2 Jiggers Brandy
4 Dashes Curaçao
1 Egg White

Shake well with ice and strain into glass. Serve with a grating of Nutmeg.

Bosom Caresser

2/3 Brandy
1/3 Curaçao
1 Teaspoon Grenadine
1 Egg Yolk

Shake well with ice and strain into glass.

Brandy

2 Jiggers Brandy
1/2 Jigger Curaçao
1 Dash Angostura Bitters

Stir well with ice and strain into glass. Serve with twist of Lemon Peel.

Brandy Blazer

2 Jiggers Brandy
1 Small Twist Orange Peel
1 Twist Lemon Peel
1 Lump Sugar

Place Sugar in bottom of shaker and add other ingredients. Stir with a long spoon; blaze for a few seconds and extinguish. Strain into glass. Serve after dinner.

Brandy Gump

2 Jiggers Brandy
2 Dashes Grenadine
Juice of 1/2 Lemon

Shake well with ice and strain into glass.

Brandy Old-Fashioned

Place lump of Sugar in bottom of Old - Fashioned glass. Sprinkle with 1 dash Angostura Bitters. Add twist of Lemon Peel and ice cubes and fill as desired with Brandy. Stir and serve.

Brandy Sour

1-1/2 Jiggers Brandy
Juice of 1/2 Lemon
1 Teaspoon Sugar

Shake well with ice and strain and serve in a Delmonico glass. Add a Cherry and, if you want, a twist of Lemon Peel.

Brandy Special

2 Jiggers Brandy
2 Dashes Curaçao
2 Dashes Sugar Syrup
2 Dashes Bitters
1 Twist of Lemon Peel

Stir with ice and strain into glass.

Brandy Vermouth

3/4 Brandy
1/4 Sweet Vermouth
1 Dash Angostura Bitters

Stir well with ice and strain into glass.

Carrol

2/3 Brandy
1/3 Sweet Vermouth

Stir well with ice and strain into glass. The recipe calls for a pickled Walnut or Onion. But why?

Cecil Pick-Me-Up

2 Jiggers Brandy
1 Teaspoon Sugar
1 Egg Yolk

Shake well with ice, strain into large cocktail glass and fill with iced Champagne.

Ceylon (for 6)

3 Jiggers Brandy
1-1/2 Jiggers Dry Vermouth
1 Jigger Triple Sec
3 Jiggers Dry Sherry
Juice of 1/2 Lemon
1 Stick of Cinnamon, Broken

Shake well with ice and strain into glasses.

Champs Elysées (for 6)

6 Jiggers Cognac
2 Jiggers Yellow Chartreuse
2 Jiggers Lemon Juice
1 Tablespoon Powdered Sugar
1 Dash Angostura Bitters

Shake well with ice and strain into glasses.

Charles

1/2 Brandy
1/2 Sweet Vermouth
1 Dash Angostura or Orange Bitters

Stir well with ice and strain into glass.

Cherry Blossom (for 6)

5 Jiggers Brandy
4 Jiggers Cherry Brandy
1 Tablespoon Curaçao
1 Tablespoon Lemon Juice
1 Tablespoon Grenadine

Shake thoroughly with shaved ice and strain into glasses.

Chicago

1 Jigger Brandy
1 Dash Curaçao
1 Dash Angostura Bitters

Stir well with ice and strain into glass frosted with Sugar. Fill with iced Champagne.

City Slicker

2/3 Brandy
1/3 Curaçao
1 Dash Pernod

Shake well with ice and strain into glass.

Classic

1/2 Brandy
1/6 Curaçao
1/6 Maraschino
1/6 Lemon Juice

Stir well with ice and strain

into glass frosted with Sugar. Squeeze Lemon Peel over top.

Coffee No. 1

1/3 Brandy
1/3 Cointreau
1/3 Cold Black Coffee

Shake well with ice and strain into glass. May be served after dinner.

Coffee No. 2

2/3 Brandy
1/3 Port
2 Dashes Curaçao
2 Dashes Sugar Syrup
1 Egg Yolk

Shake well with ice and strain into small glass. Serve with a grating of Nutmeg. This cocktail has no Coffee in it but if properly made it should be coffee colored.

Cold Deck

1/2 Brandy
1/4 Sweet Vermouth
1/4 White Crème de Menthe

Stir well with ice and strain into glass.

Coronation No. 2

2/3 Brandy
1/3 Curaçao
1 Dash Peach Bitters
1 Dash White Crème de Menthe

Stir well with ice and strain into glass.

Corpse Reviver No. 1

1/2 Brandy
1/4 Calvados or Apple Brandy
1/4 Sweet Vermouth

Stir well with ice and strain into glass.

Cuban No. 1

2/3 Brandy
1/3 Apricot Brandy
Juice of 1/2 Lemon

Stir well with ice and strain into glass.

Davis Brandy

2/3 Brandy
1/3 Dry Vermouth
4 Dashes Grenadine
1 Dash Angostura Bitters

Stir well with ice and strain into glass.

Deauville

1/4 Brandy
1/4 Calvados or Apple Brandy
1/4 Cointreau
1/4 Lemon Juice

Stir well with ice and strain into glass.

Depth-Charge Brandy (for 6)

5 Jiggers Brandy
5 Jiggers Calvados or Apple Brandy
4 Teaspoons Grenadine
3 Tablespoons Lemon Juice

Shake gently with ice and strain into glasses.

Diabolo (for 6)

6 Jiggers Brandy
6 Jiggers Dry Vermouth
1 Teaspoon Angostura Bitters
2 Teaspoons Orange Bitters

Shake well with ice and strain into glasses. Serve with twists of Lemon Peel or, if preferred, Cherries.

Don't Go Near the Water

1/2 Brandy
1/6 Curaçao
1/6 Maraschino
1/6 Lemon Juice

Shake well with ice and strain into glass frosted with Sugar. Serve with twist of Lemon Peel.

Double Trouble

2/3 Brandy
1/3 Dry Vermouth
4 Dashes Grenadine
1 Dash Angostura Bitters

Shake well with ice and strain into glass.

Dream

2/3 Brandy
1/3 Curaçao
1 Dash Pernod

Stir well with ice and strain into glass.

East India

3/4 Brandy
1/8 Pineapple Juice
1/8 Curaçao
1 Dash Angostura Bitters

Stir well with ice and strain into glass.

Egg Sour

1 Jigger Brandy
1 Jigger Curaçao
Juice of 1/2 Lemon
1 Egg
1 Teaspoon Sugar

Shake well with ice and strain into Delmonico glass.

Etchings (for 6)

3 Jiggers Brandy
3 Jiggers Cherry Brandy
1 Tablespoon Curaçao
1 Tablespoon Lemon Juice
1 Tablespoon Grenadine

Shake with shaved ice and strain into glasses. This is very similar to CHERRY BLOSSOM.

Fancy (for 6)

10 Jiggers Cognac
2 Teaspoons Angostura Bitters

Frost rim of glass with Lemon and Sugar. Shake ingredients thoroughly with ice. Strain into glasses and fill with iced Champagne.

Flying Fortress

1 Jigger Cognac
1/3 Jigger Cointreau
1/3 Jigger Anisette
2/3 Jigger Vodka

Shake well with ice and strain into a large glass.

Frank Sullivan

1/4 Brandy
1/4 Cointreau
1/4 Lillet
1/4 Lemon Juice

Shake well with ice and strain into glass.

Froupe

1/2 Brandy
1/2 Sweet Vermouth
1 Teaspoon Benedictine

Stir well with ice and strain into glass.

Gazette

1/2 Brandy
1/2 Sweet Vermouth
1 Teaspoon Lemon Juice
1 Teaspoon Sugar Syrup

Stir well with ice and strain into glass.

Grenadier

2/3 Brandy
1/3 Ginger Brandy
1 Dash Jamaica Ginger
1 Teaspoon Powdered Sugar

Stir well with ice and strain into glass.

Harry's Pick-Me-Up

2 Jiggers Cognac
1 Teaspoon Grenadine
Juice of 1/2 Lemon

Shake well with ice and strain into glass. Fill with iced Champagne.

Harvard

1/2 Brandy
1/2 Sweet Vermouth
2 Dashes Angostura Bitters
1 Dash Sugar Syrup

Stir well with ice and strain into glass.

Hoop La

1/4 Brandy
1/4 Lemon Juice
1/4 Cointreau
1/4 Lillet

Stir well with ice and strain into glass.

Ichbien

3/4 Brandy
1/4 Curaçao
1 Egg Yolk
Milk as desired

Shake well with ice and strain into glass. Sprinkle with Nutmeg. Excellent for the morning after.

Iris (for 6)

4 Jiggers Brandy
1 Jigger Sweet Vermouth
Juice of 1 Lemon

Shake well with ice and strain into glasses.

Janet Howard

2 Jiggers Brandy
1 Dash Angostura Bitters
1 Teaspoon Orgeat Syrup

Place cube of ice in cocktail glass and add ingredients. Stir with a spoon and serve with twist of Lemon Peel.

Lady Be Good

1/2 Brandy
1/4 White Crème de Menthe
1/4 Sweet Vermouth

Shake with cracked ice and strain into glass.

Let's Slide

1/2 Brandy
1/4 Port
1/4 Blackberry Brandy

Shake well with ice and strain into glass.

Lugger

1/2 Brandy
1/2 Calvados or Apple Brandy
1 Dash Apricot Brandy

Stir with ice and strain into glass. Serve with twist of Orange Peel.

Mabel Tea (for 6)

4 Jiggers Brandy
1/2 Jigger Amer Picon
Juice of 1 Lime

Shake well with ice and strain into glasses.

Metropolitan

1/2 Brandy
1/2 Sweet Vermouth
2 Dashes Sugar Syrup
1 Dash Angostura Bitters

Stir well with ice and strain into glass.

Mikado

1 Jigger Brandy
2 Dashes Curaçao
2 Dashes Orgeat Syrup
2 Dashes Crème de Noyau
2 Dashes Angostura Bitters

Stir well with ice and strain into glass.

Moonraker

1/3 Brandy
1/3 Peach Brandy
1/3 Quinquina
3 Dashes Pernod

Shake well with ice and strain into glass.

Morning

1/2 Brandy
1/2 Dry Vermouth
2 Dashes Pernod
2 Dashes Maraschino
2 Dashes Curaçao
2 Dashes Orange Bitters

Stir well with ice and strain into glass. Squeeze Lemon Peel over top and serve with a Cherry.

Mrs. Solomon

1 Jigger Brandy
2 Dashes Curaçao
2 Dashes Angostura Bitters

Stir with ice and strain into glass frosted with Sugar. Serve with twist of Lemon Peel.

Netherland

Prepare same as MRS. SOLOMON, but use Orange Bitters.

Newton's Special

3/4 Brandy
1/4 Cointreau
1 Dash Angostura Bitters

Stir well with ice and strain into glass.

Nick's Own

1/2 Brandy
1/2 Sweet Vermouth
1 Dash Angostura Bitters
1 Dash Pernod

Stir well with ice and strain into glass. Squeeze Lemon Peel over top and serve with a Cherry.

Nicolaski

Chill 1 or 2 jiggers Brandy with ice. Pour into cocktail glass and add 1 slice Lemon dipped in Powdered Sugar.

Night Cap

1/3 Brandy
1/3 Curaçao
1/3 Anisette
1 Egg Yolk

Shake well with ice and strain into glass.

None but the Brave

2/3 Brandy
1/3 Pimento Dram
1 Teaspoon Powdered Sugar
1 Dash of Jamaica Ginger
1 Dash Lemon Juice

Shake well with ice and strain into glass.

Normandy (for 6)

3 Jiggers Brandy
2 Jiggers Calvados or Apple Brandy
1 Jigger Dry Gin
4 Jiggers Sweet Cider

Shake well with ice and strain into glasses.

Odd McIntyre

1/4 Brandy
1/4 Cointreau
1/4 Lillet
1/4 Lemon Juice

Stir well with ice and strain into glass.

Olympic

1/3 Brandy
1/3 Curaçao
1/3 Orange Juice

Stir well with ice and strain into glass.

Panama

Prepare same as ALEXANDER No. 2.

Peppermint Stick

1 Jigger Brandy
3 Dashes Curaçao
1 Dash Peach Bitters
1 Dash Peppermint

Shake well with ice and strain into glass.

Peter Tower

2/3 Brandy
1/3 Light Rum
1 Teaspoon Grenadine
1 Teaspoon Curaçao
1 Teaspoon Lemon Juice

Shake well with ice and strain into glass.

Phoebe Snow

1/2 Brandy
1/2 Dubonnet
1 Dash Pernod

Stir well with ice and strain into glass.

Poop Deck (see Let's Slide)

Prairie Oyster No. 1

1 Jigger Brandy
1 Egg
1 Dash Worcestershire Sauce
Salt if desired

Carefully break egg into 6 ounce glass. Add Worcestershire Sauce and Brandy. Blend lightly with Egg White, keeping Yolk intact. Take!

Presto

2/3 Brandy
1/3 Sweet Vermouth
1 Dash Orange Juice
1 Dash Pernod

Stir well with ice and strain into glass.

Quaker's

1/3 Brandy
1/3 Rum
1/6 Lemon Juice
1/6 Raspberry Syrup

Shake well with ice and strain into glass.

Queen Elizabeth

1/2 Brandy
1/2 Sweet Vermouth
1 Dash Curaçao

Stir well with ice and strain into glass. Add a Cherry if desired.

Quelle Vie

2/3 Brandy
1/3 Kümmel

Stir well with ice and strain into glass.

Ray Long

1-1/2 Jiggers Brandy
3/4 Jigger Sweet Vermouth
4 Dashes Pernod
1 Dash Angostura Bitters

Stir well with ice and strain into glass.

Rock-a-Bye (same as Froupe)

Saratoga No. 1

2 Jiggers Brandy
2 Dashes Maraschino
2 Dashes Angostura Bitters
1/4 Slice Pineapple

Shake well with ice and strain. Add a little Soda Water if desired.

Saucy Sue

1/2 Brandy
1/2 Calvados or Apple Brandy
1 Dash Apricot Brandy
1 Dash Pernod

Stir well with ice and strain into glass. Squeeze Orange Peel over top.

Savoy Hotel

1/3 Brandy
1/3 Benedictine
1/3 Crème de Cacao

Pour ingredients carefully into liqueur glass so that they do not mix. Serve after dinner.

Sidecar

1/2 Brandy
1/4 Cointreau
1/4 Lemon Juice

Shake well with ice and strain into glass.

Sink or Swim

3/4 Brandy
1/4 Sweet Vermouth
1 Dash Angostura Bitters

Stir well with ice and strain into glass.

Sir Ridgeway Knight

2/3 Jigger Brandy
2/3 Jigger Triple Sec
2/3 Jigger Yellow Chartreuse
2 Dashes Angostura Bitters

Shake well with ice and strain into glass.

Sir Walter

2/3 Brandy
1/3 Light Rum
1 Teaspoon Grenadine
1 Teaspoon Curaçao
1 Teaspoon Lemon Juice

Shake well with ice and strain into glass.

Sledge Hammer

1/3 Brandy
1/3 Rum
1/3 Apple Brandy
1 Dash Pernod

Shake well with ice and strain into glass.

Sleepy Head

2 Jiggers Brandy
1 Twist Orange Peel
4 Leaves Fresh Mint, slightly crushed
1–2 Cubes Ice

Combine in Old-Fashioned glass and fill with ginger ale.

Stinger

1/2 Brandy
1/2 White Crème de Menthe

Shake well with shaved ice and strain into glass.

Stomach Reviver

1/3 Brandy
1/3 Kümmel
1/6 Angostura Bitters
1/6 Fernet Branca

Stir well with ice and strain into glass.

Sweeney's

1 Jigger Brandy
1/3 Jigger Pineapple Juice
1 Dash Maraschino
3 Dashes Angostura Bitters

Shake well with ice and strain into glass.

Tantalus

1/3 Brandy
1/3 Forbidden Fruit Liqueur
1/3 Lemon Juice

Shake well with ice and strain into glass.

The Devil

2/3 Jigger Brandy
2/3 Jigger Green Crème de Menthe
1 Pinch Red Pepper

Shake Brandy and Crème de Menthe and strain into glass. Sprinkle Red Pepper on top.

Third Rail No. 2

1/3 Brandy
1/3 Calvados or Apple Brandy
1/3 Light Rum
1 Dash Pernod

Shake well with ice and strain into glass.

Three Miller

2/3 Brandy
1/3 Light Rum
1 Dash Lemon Juice
1 Teaspoon Grenadine

Stir well with ice and strain.

Thunder or Thunder and Lightning

2 Jiggers Brandy
1 Teaspoon Sugar Syrup
1 Egg Yolk
1 Pinch Cayenne Pepper

Shake well with ice and strain into glass.

Tin Wedding

3/4 Jigger Brandy
3/4 Dry Gin
3/4 Sweet Vermouth
2 Dashes Orange Bitters

Shake well with ice and strain into glass.

Vanderbilt Hotel

3/4 Brandy
1/4 Cherry Brandy
2 Dashes Angostura Bitters
2 Dashes Sugar Syrup

Stir well with ice and strain into glass.

Wallick's Special

1 Jigger Brandy
1 Jigger Cream
1 Egg White
1/2 Teaspoon Powdered Sugar
2 Dashes Grenadine

Shake well with ice and strain into glass.

Ward's

1/2 Jigger Brandy
1/2 Jigger Chartreuse
1 Twist Orange Peel

Arrange the Orange Peel in bottom of glass to form a circle. Fill it with finely cracked ice and add the Chartreuse and Brandy and decorate with Fresh Mint leaves. Different Liqueurs may be used if desired.

Waterbury

2 Jiggers Brandy
1 Egg White
Juice of 1/4 Lemon
1/2 Teaspoon Powdered Sugar
2 Dashes Grenadine

Shake well with ice and strain into glass.

W.C.T.U. (for 6)

4-1/2 Jiggers Brandy
4-1/2 Jiggers Dry Vermouth
1 Teaspoon Angostura Bitters
1 Teaspoon Orange Bitters

Shake quickly with shaved ice and strain into glasses. Serve with a twist of Lemon Peel.

Whip

1/2 Brandy
1/4 Sweet Vermouth
1/4 Dry Vermouth
3 Dashes Curaçao
1 Dash Pernod

Shake well with ice and strain into glass.

White Way No. 1

1/3 Brandy
1/3 Anisette
1/3 Pernod

Stir well with ice and strain into glass.

Why Marry

3/8 Brandy
1/8 Dry Gin
1/8 Cointreau
1/8 Lemon Juice

Shake well with ice and strain into glass.

William of Orange

2/3 Brandy
1/3 Curaçao
1/3 Orange Bitters

Stir well with ice and strain into glass.

Willie Smith

2/3 Brandy
1/3 Maraschino
1 Dash Lemon Juice

Stir well with ice and strain into glass.

W. Johnson Quinn

1/2 Brandy
1/4 Sweet Vermouth
1/4 Dry Vermouth
3 Dashes Curaçao
1 Dash Grenadine

Stir well with ice and strain into glass.

Yes and No

2 Jiggers Brandy
4 Dashes Curaçao
1 Egg White

Shake well with ice and strain into glass. Sprinkle with grating of Nutmeg.

Young Man

3/4 Brandy
1/4 Sweet Vermouth
2 Dashes Curaçao
1 Dash Angostura Bitters

Stir well with ice and strain into glass.

Zoom

1-1/2 Jiggers Brandy
1/3 Jigger Honey
1/2 Jigger Cream

Shake with ice and strain into glass.

CALVADOS, APPLEJACK OR APPLE BRANDY BASE

A. J.

1/2 Applejack
1/2 Unsweetened Grape-fruit Juice
Grenadine to taste

Shake well with ice and strain into glass.

Ante

1/2 Calvados or Apple Brandy
1/4 Cointreau
1/4 Dubonnet
1 Dash Angostura Bitters

Stir well with ice and strain into glass.

Apple

1/3 Calvados or Apple Brandy
1/6 Brandy
1/6 Gin
1/3 Sweet Cider

Stir well with ice and strain into glass.

Applejack No. 1

1 Jigger Applejack
1 Teaspoon Sugar Syrup
2 Dashes Orange Bitters
1 Dash Angostura Bitters

Stir well with ice and strain into glass.

Applejack No. 2

3/4 Calvados or Apple Brandy
1/4 Sweet Vermouth
1 Dash Angostura Bitters

Stir well with ice and strain into glass.

Applejack Rabbit

1 Jigger Applejack or Apple Brandy
1/3 Jigger Lemon Juice
1/3 Jigger Orange Juice
Maple Syrup to taste

Shake well with ice and strain into glass.

Applejack Sour

2 Jiggers Applejack
Juice of 1/2 Lime
Juice of 1/2 Lemon
1 Dash Grenadine
1/2 Teaspoon Sugar

Shake well with ice and strain into Delmonico glass. Decorate with fruit if desired.

Barton Special

1/2 Calvados or Apple Brandy
1/4 Scotch Whisky
1/4 Dry Gin

Shake well with ice and strain into glass. Serve with twist of Lemon Peel.

Bentley

1/2 Calvados or Apple Brandy
1/2 Dubonnet

Stir well with ice and strain into glass.

B.V.D.

Prepare same as APPLEJACK No. 2, omitting Bitters. Serve with twist of Lemon Peel.

Calvados

1/3 Calvados or Apple Brandy
1/3 Orange Juice
1/6 Cointreau
1/6 Orange Bitters

Stir well with ice and strain into glass.

Castle Dip

1/2 Apple Brandy
1/2 White Crème de Menthe
3 Dashes Pernod

Shake well with ice and strain into glass.

Depth Bomb

1 Jigger Applejack
1 Jigger Brandy
1/4 Teaspoon Grenadine
1/4 Teaspoon Lemon Juice

Shake well with ice and strain into glass.

Dick Molnar or Diki-Diki

2/3 Calvados or Apple Brandy
1/6 Swedish Punch
1/6 Grapefruit Juice

Stir well with ice and strain into glass.

Honeymoon

1 Jigger Applejack
1/2 Jigger Benedictine
Juice of 1/2 Lemon
3 Dashes Curaçao

Shake well with ice and strain into glass.

Jack-in-the-Box

1 Jigger Applejack
1/2 Jigger Pineapple Juice
Juice of 1/2 Lemon
2 Dashes Angostura Bitters

Shake well with ice and strain into glass.

Jack Rose

1 Jigger Applejack
1/3 Jigger Grenadine
Juice of 1/2 Lime

Shake well with ice and strain into glass.

Jersey Lightning

2 Jiggers Applejack
1 Dash Angostura Bitters
Sugar Syrup to taste

Shake well with ice and strain into glass.

Kenny (for 4)

3 Jiggers Applejack
2 Jiggers Sweet Vermouth
Juice of 1/2 Lemon
1 Dash Angostura Bitters
2 Dashes Grenadine

Shake well with ice and strain into glasses.

Liberty

2/3 Applejack
1/3 Light Rum
1 Dash Sugar Syrup

Shake well with ice and strain into glass.

Oom Paul

1/2 Calvados or Apple Brandy
1/2 Dubonnet
1 Dash Angostura Bitters

Stir well with ice and strain into glass.

Philadelphia Scotchman

1/3 Applejack
1/3 Port
1/3 Orange Juice

Place in large cocktail glass with cracked ice and fill with Soda Water.

Princess Mary's Pride

1/2 Calvados or Apple Brandy
1/4 Dubonnet
1/4 Dry Vermouth

Stir well with ice and strain into glass.

Roulette

1/2 Calvados or Apple Brandy
1/4 Light Rum
1/4 Swedish Punch

Stir well with ice and strain into glass.

Royal Smile

1/2 Applejack
1/4 Dry Gin
1/4 Grenadine
Juice of 1/4 Lemon

Shake well with ice and strain into glass.

Sharky Punch

3/4 Calvados or Apple Brandy
1/4 Rye Whiskey
1 Teaspoon Sugar Syrup

Shake well with ice and strain into glass. Add dash of Soda Water.

Special Rough

1/2 Applejack
1/2 Brandy
1 Dash Pernod

Stir with shaved ice and strain into glass.

Star No. 1

1/2 Applejack
1/2 Sweet Vermouth
1 Dash Orange Bitters

Stir with cracked ice and strain into glass. Sugar Syrup may be added if desired.

Stone Fence No. 1

2 Jiggers Applejack
1–2 Dashes Angostura Bitters

Place in tall glass with ice and fill with Cider.

Tinton

2/3 Applejack
1/3 Port Wine

Stir well with ice and strain into glass.

Torpedo

2/3 Calvados or Apple Brandy
1/3 Brandy
1 Dash Gin

Stir well with ice and strain into glass.

Tulip

1/3 Calvados or Apple Brandy
1/3 Sweet Vermouth
1/6 Apricot Brandy
1/6 Lemon Juice

Stir well with ice and strain into glass.

Twelve Miles Out

1/3 Calvados or Apple Brandy
1/3 Light Rum
1/3 Swedish Punch

Stir well with ice and strain into glass. Squeeze Orange Peel over top.

Whist

1/2 Calvados or Apple Brandy
1/4 Light Rum
1/4 Sweet Vermouth

Stir well with ice and strain into glass.

Widow's Kiss

1/2 Calvados or Apple Brandy
1/4 Yellow Chartreuse
1/4 Benedictine
1 Dash Angostura Bitters

Shake well with ice and strain into glass.

COCKTAILS

GIN BASE

Abbey

1/2 Dry Gin
1/4 Lillet
1/4 Orange Juice
1 Dash Angostura Bitters

Stir well with ice and strain into glass. Serve with a twist of Orange Peel or Cherry.

Alaska

3/4 Dry Gin
1/4 Yellow Chartreuse
2 Dashes Orange Bitters

Stir well with ice and strain into glass. Serve with a twist of Lemon Peel.

Alexander No. 2

1/2 Dry Gin
1/4 Crème de Cacao
1/4 Cream

Shake well with ice and strain into glass. (See Index for Alexander No. 1 with Brandy Base.)

Alexander's Sister

1/2 Dry Gin
1/4 Crème de Menthe
1/4 Cream

Shake well with ice and strain into glass.

Alfonso Special

1/4 Dry Gin
1/4 Dry Vermouth
1/2 Grand Marnier
4 Dashes Sweet Vermouth
1 Dash Angostura Bitters

Shake well with ice and strain into glass.

Allen Special

2/3 Dry Gin
1/3 Maraschino
1 Dash Lemon Juice

Stir well with ice and strain into glass.

Allies

1/2 Dry Gin
1/2 Dry Vermouth
2 Dashes Kümmel

Stir well with ice and strain into glass.

Almond or a Young Girl's Fancy (for approximately 6)

Warm 2 jiggers of Dry Gin slightly and add to it 1 teaspoon Powdered Sugar, 6 peeled Almonds and, if you can find one, a crushed peach kernel. Let stand till cool, then add:

1/3 Jigger Kirsch
1/3 Jigger Peach Brandy
2 Jiggers Dry Vermouth
4 Jiggers Sweet White Wine

Shake well with ice and strain into glasses.

Angel Face

1/3 Dry Gin
1/3 Apricot Brandy
1/3 Calvados or Apple Brandy

Stir well with ice and strain into glass.

Apparent

1/2 Dry Gin
1/2 Dubonnet
1 Dash Pernod

Shake well with ice and strain into glass.

Appetizer No. 2 or Dubonnet

1/2 Dry Gin
1/2 Dubonnet

Stir well with ice and strain into glass. The juice of 1/2 Orange or a dash of Angostura Bitters may be added if desired.

Apricot (dry) (for 6)

2 Jiggers Dry Gin
2 Jiggers Dry Vermouth
1-1/2 Jiggers Cognac
2–3 Jiggers Peach Bitters
2 Apricots

Cut the Apricots in half and let them soak in the Cognac with their crushed kernels for 2 hours. Add the remaining ingredients, shake well with ice and strain into glasses.

Apricot (sweet) (for 6)

1 Teaspoon Apricot Jam
1 Jigger Abricotine
2 Jiggers Dry Gin
2-1/2 Jiggers Dry Vermouth
2 Dashes Peach Bitters

Stir the jam into the Abricotine. Add the remaining ingredients and pour into shaker. Place the shaker on ice and leave till cold. Add crushed ice, shake well and strain into glasses.

Artillery

2/3 Dry Gin
1/3 Sweet Vermouth
2 Dashes Bokers or Angostura Bitters

Stir well with ice and strain into glass. Serve with a twist of Lemon Peel.

Astoria

2/3 Dry Gin
1/3 Dry Vermouth
1 Dash Orange Bitters

Stir well with ice and strain into glass. Serve with an Olive.

Atta Boy

2/3 Dry Gin
1/3 Dry Vermouth
4 Dashes Grenadine

Stir well with ice and strain into glass. Serve with a twist of Lemon Peel.

Attention

1/4 Dry Gin
1/4 Pernod
1/4 Dry Vermouth
1/4 Crème de Violette
2 Dashes Orange Bitters

Stir well with ice and strain into glass.

Atty

3/4 Dry Gin
1/4 Dry Vermouth
3 Dashes Crème de Violette

Stir well with ice and strain into glass. Serve with a twist of Lemon Peel. A dash or two of Pernod also may be added.

Aviation

2/3 Dry Gin
1/3 Lemon Juice
2 Dashes Maraschino
2 Dashes Apricot Brandy

Stir well with ice and strain into glass.

Barbary Coast

1/4 Dry Gin
1/4 Scotch Whisky
1/4 Crème de Cacao
1/4 Cream

Shake well with ice and strain into small highball or Old-Fashioned glass.

Barking Dog

1/3 Dry Gin
1/3 Dry Vermouth
1/3 Sweet Vermouth
2 Dashes Calisay

Stir well with ice and strain into glass. Serve with a Cherry.

Barnum

2/3 Dry Gin
1/3 Apricot Brandy
2 Dashes Angostura Bitters
1 Dash Lemon or Lime Juice

Shake well with ice and strain into glass.

Baron

2/3 Dry Gin
1/3 Dry Vermouth
6 Dashes Curaçao
2 Dashes Sweet Vermouth

Stir well with ice and strain into glass. Serve with a twist of Lemon Peel.

Bass Wyatt (for 6)

4 Beaten Eggs
4 Jiggers Dry Gin
2/3 Jigger Cherry Brandy or Curaçao
1/2 Teaspoon Orange Bitters
Vanilla to taste

Shake well with ice and strain into glasses frosted with Sugar. Serve with a grating of Nutmeg on each.

Beauty Spot

2/3 Gin
1/3 Grenadine
1 Egg White

Shake well with ice and strain into glass.

Bees' Knees

1 Jigger Gin
1 Teaspoon Honey
Juice of 1/4 Lemon

Shake well with ice and strain into glass.

Belmont

2/3 Gin
1/3 Grenadine or Raspberry Syrup
1/2 Jigger Cream

Shake well with ice and strain into glass.

Bennett

3/4 Dry Gin
1/4 Lime Juice
1–2 Dashes Angostura Bitters
1 Teaspoon Powdered Sugar (optional)

Shake well with ice and strain into glass.

Bermuda Rose

1 Jigger Dry Gin
1 Dash Grenadine
1 Dash Apricot Brandy
1/3 Jigger Lemon or Lime Juice

Shake well with ice and strain into glass.

Berry Wall

1/2 Dry Gin
1/2 Sweet Vermouth
4 Dashes Curaçao

Stir with ice and strain into glass. Twist a Lemon Peel just over the top and serve with a Cherry.

Best Home-Made

1–2 Jiggers Gin
Juice of 1/2 Orange

Shakc well with ice and strain into glass.

Bich's Special

2/3 Dry Gin
1/3 Lillet
1 Dash Angostura Bitters

Stir well with ice and strain into glass. Squeeze Orange Peel over top.

Biffy

1/2 Dry Gin
1/4 Swedish Punch
1/4 Lemon Juice

Stir well with ice and strain into glass.

Bijou

1/3 Dry Gin
1/3 Green Chartreuse
1/3 Sweet Vermouth
1 Dash Orange Bitters

Stir well with ice and strain into glass. Serve with a twist of Lemon Peel.

Bill Lyken's Delight

1/2 Dry Gin
1/2 Sweet Vermouth
4 Dashes Curaçao
1 Twist Lemon Peel
1 Twist Orange Peel

Stir well with ice and strain into glass.

Bitter

1/2 Dry Gin
1/4 Lemon Juice
1/4 Green Chartreuse
1 Dash Pernod

Shake well with ice and strain into glass. A pinch of Sugar may be added if desired.

Blackthorn

1/2 Sloe Gin
1/2 Sweet Vermouth
2 Dashes Orange Bitters

Stir well with ice and strain into glass. Twist Lemon Peel over top and serve with a Cherry.

Blenton

2/3 English Gin
1/3 Dry Vermouth
1 Dash Angostura Bitters

Stir well with ice and strain into glass. Twist Lemon Peel over top and serve with a Cherry.

Bloodhound

1/2 Dry Gin
1/4 Dry Vermouth
1/4 Sweet Vermouth
2–3 Crushed Strawberries

Stir well with ice and strain into glass.

Blue Bird

2 Jiggers Dry Gin
4 Dashes Angostura Bitters
4 Dashes Curaçao

Stir well with ice and strain into glass. Twist Lemon Peel over top and serve with a Cherry.

Blue Devil

1/2 Dry Gin
1/4 Maraschino
1/4 Lemon or Lime Juice
1 Dash Blue Vegetable Extract (coloring)

Shake well with ice and strain into glass.

Blue Moon

1 Jigger Dry Gin
1/3 Jigger Maraschino
1 Egg White

Shake well with ice and strain into glass.

Blue Train

1/2 Dry Gin
1/4 Lemon Juice
1/4 Cointreau
1 Dash Blue Vegetable Extract (coloring)

Shake well with ice and strain into glass.

Bon Appetit

1/2 Dry Gin
1/2 Dubonnet
3 Dashes Angostura Bitters
Juice of 1/2 Orange

Shake well with ice and strain into glass.

Breakfast

2/3 Dry Gin
1/3 Grenadine
1 Egg White

Shake well with ice and strain into glass.

Bronx (dry)

3/4 Dry Gin
1/4 Dry Vermouth
Juice of 1/4 Orange

Stir well with ice and strain into glass.

Bronx (sweet)

1/2 Dry Gin
1/4 Dry Vermouth
1/4 Sweet Vermouth
Juice of 1/4 Orange

Stir well with ice and strain into glass.

Bronx Golden

Follow directions for BRONX (sweet) adding Yolk of 1 Egg.

Bronx River (for 3)

3 Jiggers Dry Gin
1 Jigger Sweet Vermouth
Juice of 1 Lemon
1/2 Teaspoon Sugar

Stir well with ice and strain into glasses.

Bronx Silver or Oriental

Follow directions for BRONX (sweet) adding the

White of 1 Egg and 1 slice Pineapple.

Buby

1/2 Dry Gin
1/2 Lemon Juice
1 Teaspoon Grenadine

Shake well and strain into glass.

Bulldog

Place 2–3 cubes in a large Old-Fashioned glass. Add 2 jiggers Gin, the juice of 1 Orange and fill with Ginger Ale. Stir slightly and serve . . . sometimes with a straw.

Bunny Hug

1/3 Dry Gin
1/3 Whiskey (Bourbon or Blend)
1/3 Pernod

Shake well with ice and strain into glass.

B.V.D.

1/3 Dry Gin
1/3 Light Rum
1/3 Dry Vermouth

Stir well with ice and strain into glass.

Cabaret

1/2 Dry Gin
1/2 Dubonnet
1 Dash Pernod
1 Dash Angostura Bitters

Stir well with ice and strain into glass. Serve with a Cherry.

Café de Paris

2 Jiggers Dry Gin
3 Dashes Anisette
1 Teaspoon Cream
1 Egg White

Shake well with ice and strain into glass.

Campden

1/2 Dry Gin
1/4 Cointreau
1/4 Lillet

Stir well with ice and strain into glass. Serve with a Cherry.

Caruso

1/3 Dry Gin
1/3 Dry Vermouth
1/3 Green Crème de Menthe

Stir well with ice and strain into glass.

Casino

2 Jiggers Old Tom Gin
2 Dashes Maraschino
2 Dashes Orange Bitters
2 Dashes Lemon Juice

Stir well with ice and strain into glass.

Cat's Eye (for 6)

4 Jiggers Dry Gin
1 Jigger Lemonade
1 Jigger Water
2 Teaspoons Kirsch
1 Jigger Cointreau
3 Jiggers Dry Vermouth

Shake well with ice and strain into glasses. Serve with a twist of Lemon Peel.

C.F.H.

1/3 Dry Gin
1/6 Calvados or Apple Brandy
1/6 Swedish Punch
1/6 Grenadine
1/6 Lemon Juice

Shake well with ice and strain into glass.

Chanticleer

2 Jiggers Dry Gin
Juice of 1/2 Lemon
1 Tablespoon Raspberry Syrup
1 Egg White

Shake well with ice and strain into glass.

Chappelle

Muddle 2–3 slices of Pineapple in a shaker. Add:

1/2 Jigger Sweet Vermouth
1/2 Jigger Dry Gin
Juice of 1/2 Lime

Shake well with ice and strain into glass.

Charleston

1/6 Dry Gin
1/6 Kirsch
1/6 Maraschino
1/6 Curaçao
1/6 Dry Vermouth
1/6 Sweet Vermouth

Stir well with ice and strain into glass. Squeeze Lemon Peel over top.

Charlie Lindbergh

1/2 English Gin
1/2 Lillet
2 Dashes Apricot Brandy
2 Dashes Orange Juice

Stir well with ice and strain into glass. Squeeze Lemon Peel over top.

Chatterley

1/2 Dry Gin
1/4 Dry Vermouth
1/8 Orange Juice
1/8 Curaçao

Shake well with ice and strain into glass.

Chorus Lady

1/3 Dry Gin
1/3 Dry Vermouth
1/3 Sweet Vermouth
Juice of 1/4 Orange

Stir well with ice and strain into glass. Serve with slice of Orange and a Cherry.

Church Parade

2/3 English Gin
1/3 Dry Vermouth
1 Dash Curaçao
4 Dashes Orange Juice

Stir well with ice and strain into glass. Serve with a Cherry.

Claridge

1/3 Dry Gin
1/3 Dry Vermouth
1/6 Apricot Brandy
1/6 Cointreau

Stir well with ice and strain into glass. Serve with a Cherry.

Clover Club

2/3 Dry Gin
1/3 Grenadine
Juice of 1/2 Lime
1 Egg White

Shake well with ice and strain into glass.

Clover Leaf

Prepare same as a CLOVER CLUB but serve with a Mint Leaf in each glass.

Club

2/3 Dry Gin
1/3 Sweet Vermouth

Stir well with ice and strain into glass. Serve with a Cherry or an Olive.

Colonial

2/3 Dry Gin
1/3 Grapefruit Juice
3 Dashes Maraschino

Shake well with ice and strain into glass.

Come Again

1 Jigger Dry Gin
2 Dashes Peach Bitters
2 Sprigs Fresh Mint

Shake with shaved ice and strain into glass.

Cooperstown

1/2 Dry Gin
1/4 Dry Vermouth
1/4 Sweet Vermouth
1 Sprig Fresh Mint

Stir well with ice and strain into glass. Serve with a small sprig of Mint or a Cherry.

Cordova

2/3 Dry Gin
1/3 Sweet Vermouth
1 Dash Pernod
1 Teaspoon Cream

Shake well with ice and strain into glass.

Cornell

1 Jigger Dry Gin
3 Dashes Maraschino
1 Egg White

Shake well with ice and strain into glass.

Corpse Reviver No. 2

1/4 Dry Gin
1/4 Cointreau
1/4 Swedish Punch
1/4 Lemon Juice
1 Dash Pernod

Shake well with ice and strain into glass.

Cubano

1/2 Dry Gin
1/2 Dry Vermouth
4 Drops Kümmel
4 Drops Charbreux
2 Drops Pineapple Syrup

Shake well with ice and strain into glass.

Curaçao (for 6)

1 Jigger Gin
1 Jigger Brandy
2-1/2 Jiggers Curaçao
2-1/2 Jiggers Orange Juice

Shake well with ice and strain into glasses which have had a dash each Orange Bitters.

Damn the Weather

1/2 Dry Gin
1/4 Sweet Vermouth
1/4 Orange Juice
3 Dashes Curaçao

Shake well with ice and strain into glass.

Darb

1/3 Dry Gin
1/3 Dry Vermouth
1/3 Apricot Brandy
4 Dashes Lemon Juice

Stir well with ice and strain into glass.

Darby

1 Jigger Dry Gin
1/3 Jigger Lime Juice
1/3 Jigger Grapefruit Juice
1 Teaspoon Powdered Sugar

Shake well with ice and strain into a large cocktail glass. Top with a squirt of soda and add a Cherry.

Deep Sea

1/2 Old Tom Gin
1/2 Dry Vermouth
1 Dash Pernod
1 Dash Orange Bitters

Stir well with ice and strain into glass. Squeeze Lemon Peel over top and serve with an Olive.

Dempsey

1/2 Dry Gin
1/2 Calvados or Apple Brandy
2 Dashes Pernod
2 Dashes Grenadine

Stir well with ice and strain into glass.

Depth Charge

1/2 Dry Gin
1/2 Lillet
2 Dashes Pernod

Shake well with ice and strain into glass. Squeeze Orange Peel over top.

Derby No. 1

1 Jigger Dry Gin
2 Dashes Peach Bitters
2 Sprigs Fresh Mint

Shake well with ice and strain into glass.

Desert Healer

2 Jiggers Dry Gin
1/3 Jigger Cherry Brandy
Juice of 1 Orange

Shake well with ice and strain into tall glass. Fill with cold Ginger Beer.

Devonia (for 6)

4 Jiggers Dry Gin
8 Jiggers Sparkling Cider
2 Dashes Orange Bitters

Stir lightly with cracked ice and strain into glasses.

D.F.

1/2 Dry Gin
1/2 Unsweetened Grapefruit Juice
Grenadine to Taste

Stir well with ice and strain into glass.

Diabola

1/3 Dry Gin
2/3 Dubonnet
2 Dashes Orgeat Syrup

Stir well with ice and strain into glass. Serve with a Cherry.

Dick Jr.

1/3 Dry Gin
1/3 Dry Vermouth
1/3 Apricot Brandy
Juice of 1 Lime

Shake well with ice and strain into glass.

Dixie

1/2 Jigger Dry Gin
1/4 Jigger Pernod
1/4 Jigger Dry Vermouth
Juice of 1/4 Orange
2 Dashes Grenadine

Shake well with ice and strain into glass.

Dodge Special

1/2 Dry Gin
1/2 Cointreau
1 Dash Grape Juice

Stir well with ice and strain into glass.

Dolly O'Dare

1/2 Dry Gin
1/2 Dry Vermouth
6 Dashes Apricot Brandy

Stir well with ice and strain into glass. Squeeze Orange Peel over top.

D.O.M.

3/4 Dry Gin
1/8 Orange Juice
1/8 Benedictine

Shake well with ice and strain into glass.

Douglas

2/3 English Gin
1/3 Dry Vermouth

Stir well with ice and strain into glass. Squeeze Orange or Lemon Peel over top.

Du Barry

2/3 English Gin
1/3 Dry Vermouth
2 Dashes Pernod
1 Dash Angostura Bitters

Stir well with ice and strain into glass. Serve with thin slice of Orange.

Dunhill's Special (for 6)

4 Jiggers Dry Gin
4 Jiggers Sherry
4 Jiggers Dry Vermouth
1 Tablespoon Curaçao

Stir well with ice and strain into glasses with 2 dashes Pernod and an Olive in each.

Eagle's Dream

3/4 Dry Gin
1/4 Crème d'Yvette
Juice of 1/4 Lemon
1 Egg White
1 Teaspoon Powdered Sugar

Shake well with ice and strain into glass.

Earthquake

1/3 Dry Gin
1/3 Whiskey
1/3 Pernod

Shake well with ice and strain into glass. It's been said by those who know that one of these should be sufficient.

Eclipse

1/3 Dry Gin
2/3 Sloe Gin

Place a Cherry or Ripe Olive in a cocktail glass and add enough Grenadine to cover. Shake the gins with ice and strain slowly into the glass so that they *do not* mix with the Grenadine. Squeeze an Orange Peel over the top.

Eddie Brown

2/3 Dry Gin
1/3 Lillet
2 Dashes Apricot Brandy

Stir well with ice and strain into glass. Squeeze Lemon Peel over top.

Elegant

1/2 Dry Gin
1/2 Dry Vermouth
2 Dashes Grand Marnier

Stir well with ice and serve.

Elk

1/2 Dry Gin
1/2 Prunelle Brandy
2 Dashes Dry Vermouth

Shake well with ice and strain into glass.

Emerald (for 6)

3 Jiggers Dry Gin
3 Jiggers Green Chartreuse

3 Jiggers Sweet Vermouth
1 Teaspoon Orange Bitters

Shake well with ice and strain into glass. Serve with a Cherry and a twist of Lemon Peel.

Empire

1/2 Dry Gin
1/4 Calvados or Apple Brandy
1/4 Apricot Brandy

Stir well with ice and strain into glass. Serve with Cherry.

E. Nos

2/3 Dry Gin
1/3 Dry Vermouth
3 Dashes Pernod

Stir well with ice and strain into glass. Serve with Cherry.

Eton Blazer

3/4 English Gin
1/4 Kirsch
1/2 Tablespoon Powdered Sugar
Juice of 1/2 Lemon

Shake well and strain into large cocktail glass. Fill with Soda.

Everything But

1/4 Dry Gin
1/4 Whiskey
1/4 Lemon Juice
1/4 Orange Juice
1 Egg
1 Teaspoon Apricot Brandy
1/2 Teaspoon Powdered Sugar

Shake well with ice and strain into glass.

Fairbanks No. 1

1/3 Dry Gin
1/3 Dry Vermouth
1/3 Apricot Brandy
1 Dash Lemon Juice
1 Dash Grenadine

Stir well with ice and strain into glass. Serve with Cherry.

Fairbanks No. 2

2/3 Dry Gin
1/3 Dry Vermouth
2 Dashes Orange Bitters
2 Dashes Crème de Noyau

Stir well with ice and strain into glass. Serve with Cherry.

Fairy Belle

3/4 Dry Gin
1/4 Apricot Brandy
1 Teaspoon Grenadine
1 Egg White

Shake well with ice and strain into glass.

Fallen Angel

2 Jiggers Dry Gin
Juice of 1 Lemon or Lime
2 Dashes Crème de Menthe
1 Dash Angostura Bitters

Stir well with ice and strain into glass. Serve with Cherry.

Fall River

1/3 Dry Gin
1/3 Brandy
1/6 White Crème de Menthe
1/6 Maraschino

Shake well with ice and strain into glass.

Fare-Thee-Well

2/3 Dry Gin
1/3 Dry Vermouth
2 Dashes Sweet Vermouth
6 Dashes Curaçao

Shake well with ice and strain into glass.

Fascinator

2/3 Dry Gin
1/3 Dry Vermouth
2 Dashes Pernod
1 Sprig Fresh Mint

Shake well with ice and strain into glass.

Favourite

1/3 Dry Gin
1/3 Dry Vermouth
1/3 Apricot Brandy
1 Dash Lemon Juice

Stir well with ice and strain into glass. Serve with Cherry

Fernet Branca

1/2 Dry Gin
1/4 Sweet Vermouth
1/4 Fernet Branca

Stir well with ice and strain into glass. Serve with Cherry.

Fifth Avenue

1/2 Dry Gin
1/4 Sweet Vermouth
1/4 Fernet Branca

Stir well with ice and strain into glass

Fifty-fifty

1/2 Dry Gin
1/2 Dry Vermouth

Stir well with cracked ice and strain into glass. Serve with Olive.

Fine and Dandy

1/2 English Gin
1/4 Cointreau
1/4 Lemon Juice
1 Dash Angostura Bitters

Stir well with ice and strain into glass. Serve with Cherry.

Fourth Degree

1/3 Dry Gin
1/3 Dry Vermouth
1/3 Sweet Vermouth
4 Dashes Pernod

Stir well with ice and strain into glass. Serve with Cherry or a twist of Lemon Peel.

Frankenjack

1/3 Dry Gin
1/3 Dry Vermouth
1/6 Apricot Brandy
1/6 Cointreau

Stir well with ice and strain into glass. Serve with Cherry.

French Rose

2/3 Jigger Dry Gin
1/3 Jigger Cherry Brandy
1/3 Jigger Cherry Liqueur

Shake well with ice and strain into glass.

Froth Blower

1 Jigger English Gin
1 Teaspoon Grenadine
1 Egg White

Shake well with ice and strain into glass.

Gasper

1/2 Dry Gin
1/2 Apricot Brandy

Add if required a very little Sugar. Shake well with ice and strain into glass.

Gene Tunney

2/3 English Gin
1/3 Dry Vermouth
1 Dash Orange Juice
1 Dash Lemon Juice

Stir well with ice and strain into glass. Serve with Cherry.

Gibson

4 Dry Gin or more
1 Dry Vermouth or less

Stir well with ice and strain into glass. Serve with a Pickled Pearl Onion.

Gilroy

1/3 Dry Gin
1/3 Cherry Brandy
1/6 Dry Vermouth
1/6 Lemon Juice
1 Dash Orange Bitters

Stir well with ice and strain into glass.

Gimblet

3/4 Dry Gin
1/4 Lime Juice

Stir well with ice and strain into glass. Fill with Soda.

Gimlet

1/2 English Gin
1/2 Rose's Lime Juice

Stir and serve in same glass. May be iced if desired.

Gin

1 Jigger Dry Gin
1 Dash Orange Bitters

Stir with cracked ice and strain into glass. Serve with twist of Lemon Peel.

Gin and Bitters

2 Jiggers Dry Gin
1 Dash Angostura Bitters

Pour over ice in glass and serve.

Gin and It

1/2 Dry Gin
1/2 Sweet Vermouth

Do not ice.

Gin and Sin

3/4 Gin
1/8 Orange Juice
1/8 Lemon Juice
1 Dash Grenadine

Shake well with ice and strain into glass.

Gin Ho or Gin-on-the-Rocks

Fill an Old-Fashioned glass with cracked ice. Pour on the amount of Gin desired and serve. A twist of Lemon Peel may be added.

Gin Sour

Prepare same as WHISKEY SOUR (see Index).

Gin Stinger

2/3 Dry Gin
1/3 White Crème de Menthe

Shake well with shaved ice and strain into glass.

Golden Clipper

1/4 Dry Gin
1/4 Light Rum
1/4 Peach Brandy
1/4 Orange Juice

Shake well with ice and strain into glass.

Golden Dawn

2/3 Jigger Dry Gin
1/2 Jigger Orange Juice
1/3 Jigger Apricot Brandy

Shake well with ice and strain into glass.

Golden Ermine

1/2 Dry Gin
3/8 Dry Vermouth
1/8 Sweet Vermouth

Stir with ice and strain into glass.

Golden Gate

1/4 Dry Gin
3/4 Orange Juice

Place in shaker and shake well without ice. Serve in tall glass.

Golf

2/3 Dry Gin
1/3 Dry Vermouth
2 Dashes Angostura Bitters

Stir well with ice and strain into glass. Serve with Olive.

Grand Royal Clover Club

2 Jiggers Dry Gin
1 Tablespoon Grenadine
Juice of 1/2 Lemon
1 Egg

Shake well with ice and strain into glass.

Grapefruit

3 Parts Dry Gin
1 Part Grapefruit Juice

Shake well with ice and strain into glass.

Grape Vine

1/2 Dry Gin
1/4 Grape Juice
1/4 Lemon Juice
1 Dash Grenadine

Stir well with ice and strain into glass.

Great Secret

2/3 Dry Gin
1/3 Lillet
1 Dash Angostura Bitters

Stir well with ice and strain into glass. Serve with twist of Orange Peel.

Green Dragon No. 1

1/2 Dry Gin
1/8 Kümmel
1/4 Crème de Menthe
1/8 Lemon Juice
4 Dashes Peach Bitters

Shake well with ice and strain into glass.

Guards

2/3 Dry Gin
1/3 Sweet Vermouth
2 Dashes Curaçao

Stir well with ice and strain into glass. Serve with twist of Orange Peel or Cherry.

Gunga Din

3/4 Dry Gin
1/4 Dry Vermouth
1 Slice Pineapple
Juice of 1/4 Orange

Shake well with ice and strain into glass.

Gypsy

1/2 English Gin
1/2 Sweet Vermouth

Stir well with ice and strain into glass. Serve with Cherry.

Hakam

1/2 Dry Gin
1/2 Sweet Vermouth
2 Dashes Curaçao
1 Dash Orange Bitters

Stir well with ice and strain into glass. Serve with Cherry.

H. and H.

2/3 Dry Gin
1/3 Lillet
2 Dashes Curaçao

Stir well with ice and strain into glass. Serve with a twist of Orange Peel.

Hanky-Panky

2/3 Dry Gin
1/3 Sweet Vermouth
2 Dashes Fernet Branca

Stir well with ice and strain into glass. Serve with twist of Orange Peel.

Harrovian

2 Jiggers Dry Gin
1 Teaspoon Orange Juice
1 Dash Lemon Juice
1 Dash Angostura Bitters

Stir well with ice and strain into glass.

Harry's

2/3 Dry Gin
1/3 Sweet Vermouth
1 Dash Pernod
2 Sprigs Fresh Mint

Shake well with ice and strain into glass. Serve with a Mint Leaf or two.

Hasty

2/3 Dry Gin
1/3 Dry Vermouth
4 Dashes Grenadine
1 Dash Pernod

Shake well with ice and strain into glass.

Have a Heart

1 Jigger Dry Gin
1/2 Jigger Swedish Punch
2 Dashes Grenadine
Juice of 1/2 Lime

Shake well with shaved ice and strain into glass. Serve with a wedge of Pineapple and a Cherry.

Hawaiian No. 1

1 Jigger Dry Gin
1/2 Jigger Pineapple Juice
1 Dash Orange Bitters
1 Egg White

Shake well with ice and strain into glass.

Hawaiian No. 2

4 Parts Dry Gin
1 Part Orange Juice
1 Part Curaçao

Shake well with ice and strain into glass.

Hoffman House (see Astoria)

Holland House

2/3 Dry Gin
1/3 Dry Vermouth
Juice of 1/4 Lemon
1 Slice Pineapple
4 Dashes Maraschino

Stir well with ice and strain into glass.

Homestead

2/3 Dry Gin
1/3 Sweet Vermouth
1 Slice Orange

Shake well with ice and strain into glass.

Honolulu

1/3 Dry Gin
1/3 Benedictine
1/3 Maraschino

Stir well with ice and strain into glass.

Hotel Plaza

1/3 Dry Gin
1/3 Dry Vermouth
1/3 Sweet Vermouth
1 Slice Pineapple

Shake well with ice and strain into glass.

H.P.W.

1/2 Old Tom Gin
1/2 Dry Vermouth

Stir well with ice and strain into glass. Serve with twist of Orange Peel.

Hugo Special

1 Jigger Dry Gin
1/2 Jigger Sweet Vermouth
2 Slices Orange
1 Slice Pineapple

Place slices of Orange and Pineapple in a mixing glass and muddle well. Add cracked ice, Gin and Vermouth. Shake well and strain into glass.

Hula-Hula

2/3 Dry Gin
1/3 Orange Juice
1 Dash Curaçao

Shake well with ice and strain into glass.

Hurricane

1/3 Dry Gin
1/3 Whiskey
1/3 Crème de Menthe
Juice of 2 Lemons

Shake well with ice and strain into glass.

Ideal

2/3 Dry Gin
1/3 Sweet Vermouth
3 Dashes Maraschino
1 Tablespoon Grapefruit Juice

Shake well with ice and strain into glass.

Imperial

1/2 Dry Gin
1/2 Dry Vermouth
1 Dash Angostura Bitters
1 Dash Maraschino

Stir well with ice and strain into glass. Serve with Olive.

Inca

1/4 Dry Gin
1/4 Sherry
1/4 Dry Vermouth
1/4 Sweet Vermouth
1 Dash Orgeat Syrup
1 Dash Orange Bitters

Stir well with ice and strain into glass.

Income Tax

1/2 Dry Gin
1/4 Dry Vermouth
1/4 Sweet Vermouth
1 Dash Angostura Bitters
Juice of 1/4 Orange

Stir well with ice and strain into glass.

Jabberwock

1/3 Dry Gin
1/3 Dry Sherry
1/3 Dubonnet
2 Dashes Orange Bitters

Stir well with ice and strain into glass. Squeeze Lemon Peel over top and serve with a Cherry.

Jack Kearns

3/4 Dry Gin
1/4 Light Rum
4 Dashes Sugar Syrup
1 Dash Lemon Juice

Shake well with ice and strain into glass. This may be made with less Sugar Syrup if desired.

Jack Pine

3/4 Dry Gin
1/4 Dry Vermouth
1 Slice Pineapple
Juice of 1/4 Orange

Shake well with ice and strain into glass.

Jack Sloat

1 Jigger Dry Gin
2 Dashes Dry Vermouth
4 Dashes Sweet Vermouth
3 Slices Pineapple

Shake well with ice and strain into glass.

Jackson

1/2 Dry Gin
1/2 Dubonnet
2 Dashes Orange Bitters

Stir well with ice and strain into glass.

Jack Withers

1/3 Dry Gin
1/3 Dry Vermouth
1/3 Sweet Vermouth
Juice of 1/2 Orange

Stir well with ice and strain.

Jewel

1/3 Dry Gin
1/3 Green Chartreuse
1/3 Sweet Vermouth
1 Dash Orange Bitters

Shake well with ice and strain into glass. Serve with twist of Lemon Peel and, if you want, a Cherry.

Jeyplak

2/3 Dry Gin
1/3 Sweet Vermouth
1 Dash Pernod

Stir well with ice and strain into glass. Twist Lemon Peel over top and serve with a Cherry.

Jimmy Blanc

2/3 Dry Gin
1/3 Lillet
3 Dashes Dubonnet

Stir well with ice and strain into glass. Squeeze Orange Peel over top.

Jockey Club

1-1/2 Jiggers Dry Gin
1 Dash Orange Bitters
1 Dash Angostura Bitters
2 Dashes Crème de Noyau
4 Dashes Lemon Juice

Stir well with ice and strain into glass.

Johnnie Mack

2/3 Sloe Gin
1/3 Curaçao
3 Dashes Pernod

Stir well with ice and strain into glass. Serve with twist of Lemon Peel.

J.O.S.

1/3 Dry Gin
1/3 Dry Vermouth
1/3 Sweet Vermouth
1 Dash Brandy
1 Dash Orange Bitters
1 Dash Lemon or Lime Juice

Stir well with ice and strain into glass. Twist Lemon Peel over top.

Journalist

2/3 Dry Gin
1/6 Dry Vermouth
1/6 Sweet Vermouth
2 Dashes Curaçao
2 Dashes Lemon Juice
1 Dash Angostura Bitters

Stir well with ice and strain into glass.

Judge Jr.

1/3 Dry Gin
1/3 Light Rum
1/3 Lemon Juice
1–3 Dashes Grenadine

Shake well with ice and strain into a glass. Powdered Sugar may be added if more sweetness is desired.

Judgette

1/3 Dry Gin
1/3 Peach Brandy
1/3 Dry Vermouth
1 Dash Lime Juice

Stir well with ice and strain. Serve with Cherry if desired.

K.C.B.

3/4 Dry Gin
1/4 Kirsch
1 Dash Apricot Brandy
1 Dash Lemon Juice

Stir well with ice and strain into glass. Serve with twist of Lemon Peel.

Kina

1/2 Dry Gin
1/4 Sweet Vermouth
1/4 Lillet

Stir well with ice and strain. Serve with Cherry if desired.

Knickerbocker

2/3 Dry Gin
1/3 Dry Vermouth
1 Dash Sweet Vermouth

Stir well with ice and strain into glass. Squeeze Lemon Peel over top.

Knockout

1/3 Dry Gin
1/3 Dry Vermouth
1/3 Pernod
1 Teaspoon White Crème de Menthe

Stir well with ice and strain into glass. Serve with Mint Leaves.

Kup's Indispensable

5/8 Dry Gin
2/8 Dry Vermouth
1/8 Sweet Vermouth
1 Dash Angostura Bitters

Stir well with ice and strain into glass. Serve with twist of Orange Peel.

Lady Finger

1/2 Dry Gin
1/4 Kirsch
1/4 Cherry Brandy

Stir well with ice and strain into glass.

Lasky

1/3 Dry Gin
1/3 Swedish Punch
1/3 Grape Juice

Shake well with ice and strain into glass.

Last Round

1/2 Dry Gin
1/2 Dry Vermouth
2 Dashes Brandy
2 Dashes Pernod

Stir well with ice and strain into glass.

Leap Frog or London Buck

1 Jigger Dry Gin
Juice of 1/2 Lemon
Cracked Ice

Place all together in a large cocktail glass and fill with Ginger Ale.

Leap Year

2/3 Dry Gin
1/6 Sweet Vermouth
1/6 Grand Marnier
1 Dash Lemon Juice

Stir well with ice and strain into glass. Squeeze Lemon Peel over top.

Leave It to Me No. 1

1/2 English Gin
1/4 Dry Vermouth
1/4 Apricot Brandy
1 Dash Lemon Juice
1 Dash Grenadine

Stir well with ice and strain into glass.

Leave It to Me No. 2

1-1/2 Jiggers Dry Gin
1 Teaspoon Raspberry Syrup
1 Teaspoon Lemon Juice
1 Dash Maraschino

Shake well with ice and strain into glass.

Leo Special

1/2 Gin
1/4 Lime Juice
1/4 Cointreau
2 Dashes Pernod

Stir well with ice and strain into glass.

Lilly

1/3 Dry Gin
1/3 Crème de Noyau
1/3 Lillet
1 Dash Lemon Juice

Stir with ice and strain into glass.

Little Devil

1/3 Dry Gin
1/3 Light Rum
1/6 Cointreau
1/6 Lemon Juice

Stir well with ice and strain into glass.

London

2/3 Dry Gin
2 Dashes Maraschino
2 Dashes Sugar Syrup
2 Dashes Orange Bitters

Stir well with ice and strain into glass. Serve with twist of Lemon Peel.

London Buck (see Leap Frog)

Lone Tree

1/3 Dry Gin
1/3 Sweet Vermouth
1/3 Dry Vermouth
2 Dashes Orange Bitters

Stir well with ice and strain into glass. Serve with Cherry.

Lord Suffolk

5/8 Dry Gin
1/8 Cointreau
1/8 Sweet Vermouth
1/8 Maraschino

Stir well with ice and strain into glass. Serve with twist of Lemon Peel.

Loud Speaker

3/8 Dry Gin
3/8 Brandy
1/8 Cointreau
1/8 Lemon Juice

Stir well with ice and strain into glass.

Luigi

1/2 Dry Gin
1/2 Dry Vermouth
Juice of 1/2 Tangerine
1 Dash Cointreau
1 Teaspoon Grenadine

Stir well with ice and strain into glass. Serve with twist of Lemon Peel.

Lutkins Special

1/2 Dry Gin
1/2 Dry Vermouth
2 Dashes Apricot Brandy
2 Dashes Orange Juice

Stir well with ice and strain into glass.

Love

1 Jigger Sloe Gin
1 Egg White
2 Dashes Lemon Juice
2 Dashes Raspberry Syrup

Shake well with ice and strain into glass.

Mabel Berra

1/2 Jigger Sloe Gin
1/2 Jigger Swedish Punch
Juice of 1/2 Lime

Shake well with ice and strain into glass.

Magnolia Blossom

1/2 Gin
1/4 Cream
1/4 Lemon Juice
1 Dash Grenadine

Shake quickly with ice and strain into glass.

Mah Jongg

2/3 Dry Gin
1/6 Light Rum
1/6 Cointreau

Stir well with ice and strain into glass. Serve with twist of Lemon Peel.

Maiden's Blush No. 1 or Maiden's Delight

2 Jiggers Dry Gin
4 Dashes Curaçao
4 Dashes Grenadine
1–2 Dashes Lemon Juice

Shake well with ice and strain into glass.

Maiden's Blush No. 2

2/3 Dry Gin
1/3 Pernod
1 Teaspoon Grenadine

Stir well with ice and strain into glass. Serve with twist of Lemon Peel.

Maiden's Prayer No. 1

3/8 Dry Gin
3/8 Cointreau
1/8 Lemon Juice
1/8 Orange Juice

Stir well with ice and strain into glass.

Maiden's Prayer No. 2

1/3 Dry Gin
1/3 Lillet
1/6 Calvados or Apple Brandy
1/6 Apricot Brandy

Stir well with ice and strain into glass.

Manyann

1/2 Dry Gin
1/2 Dubonnet
2 Dashes Curaçao
Juice of 1 Lemon

Shake well with ice and strain into glass.

Marguerite

2/3 Gin
1/3 Dry Vermouth
1 Dash Orange Bitters
1 Twist Orange Peel

Stir well with ice and strain into glass. Serve with a Cherry.

Marny

2/3 Dry Gin
1/3 Grand Marnier

Stir well with ice and strain into glass. Serve with a Cherry.

Martinez (for 6)

6 Jiggers Dry Gin
4 Jiggers Dry Vermouth
4 Teaspoons Curaçao or Maraschino
1 Teaspoon Orange Bitters

Shake with ice and strain into glasses. Serve with a twist of Lemon Peel and, if desired, a Cherry.

Martini (dry)

4 or 5 Parts Dry Gin
1 Part Dry Vermouth

Stir with ice and strain into chilled glass. Serve with twist of Lemon Peel or an Olive.

Martini (medium)

2 or 3 Parts Dry Gin
1 Part Dry Vermouth

Stir with ice and strain into chilled glass. Serve with twist of Lemon Peel or an Olive.

Martini (sweet)

3 Parts Dry Gin
1/2 Part Dry Vermouth
1/2 Part Sweet Vermouth

Stir with ice and strain into chilled glass. Serve with an Olive. A dash of Orange Bitters may be added.

Martini-on-the-Rocks

Pack an Old - Fashioned glass loosely with ice. Fill with Dry Gin and add a few dashes Dry Vermouth. Stir and serve. A twist of Lemon Peel may be added.

Martini Special (for 6)

8 Jiggers Dry Gin
3 Jiggers Sweet Vermouth
2/3 Jigger Orange Flower Water
1 Dash Angostura Bitters

Stir with ice and strain into chilled glasses. Serve with Cherries.

Maurice

1/2 Dry Gin
1/4 Sweet Vermouth
1/4 Dry Vermouth
Juice of 1/4 Orange
1 Dash Angostura Bitters

Stir well with ice and strain into glass.

Mayfair

1/2 Dry Gin
1/4 Apricot Brandy
1/4 Orange Juice
1 Dash Pimento Dram

Shake well with ice and strain into glass.

McClelland

2/3 Sloe Gin
1/3 Curaçao
1 Dash Orange Bitters

Stir well with ice and strain into glass.

Melon

1/2 Dry Gin
3/8 Maraschino
1/8 Lemon Juice

Shake well with ice and strain into glass. Serve with a Cherry.

Merry Widow

1/2 Dry Gin
1/2 Dry Vermouth
2 Dashes Benedictine
1 Dash Peychaud's Bitters
2 Dashes Pernod

Stir well with ice and strain into glass. Serve with twist of Lemon Peel.

Millionaire No. 1

2/3 Dry Gin
1/3 Pernod
1 Egg White
1 Dash Anisette

Shake well with cracked ice and strain into glass.

Million Dollar

2/3 English Gin
1/3 Sweet Vermouth

1 Tablespoon Pineapple Juice
1 Teaspoon Grenadine
1 Egg White

Shake well with ice and strain into glass.

Minnehaha

1/2 Dry Gin
1/4 Dry Vermouth
1/4 Sweet Vermouth
Juice of 1/4 Orange

Shake well with ice and strain into glass.

Mint (for 6)

4 Jiggers Dry Gin
1 Jigger Crème de Menthe
6 Jiggers White Wine
Several Sprigs of Mint

Soak the Mint for 2 hours in half the Wine. Add the other ingredients and remaining Wine. Shake well with ice and strain into glasses. Serve with a fresh sprig of Mint in each glass.

Mississippi Mule

2/3 Dry Gin
1/6 Lemon Juice
1/6 Crème de Cassis

Stir well with ice and strain into glass.

Mr. Eric Sutton's Gin Blind

6 Parts Gin
3 Parts Curaçao
2 Parts Brandy
1 Dash Orange Bitters

Stir with ice and strain into glass.

Mr. Manhattan

2 Jiggers Dry Gin
4 Dashes Orange Juice
1 Dash Lemon Juice
4 Crushed Mint Leaves
1 Lump Sugar moistened with Water

Shake well with ice and strain into glass.

Modern No. 1

2/3 Sloe Gin
1/3 Scotch Whisky
1 Dash Pernod
1 Dash Orange Bitters
1 Dash Grenadine

Shake well with ice and strain into glass.

Moll

1/3 Dry Gin
1/3 Sloe Gin
1/3 Dry Vermouth
1 Dash Orange Bitters
1/2 Teaspoon Sugar

Shake and serve.

Monkey Gland

2/3 Dry Gin
1/3 Orange Juice
3 Dashes Benedictine
3 Dashes Grenadine

Stir well with ice and strain into glass.

Monte Carlo Imperial

1/2 Dry Gin
1/4 Lemon Juice
1/4 White Crème de Menthe

Shake well with ice and strain into a large cocktail glass. Fill with Champagne.

Moonlight (for 4)

4 Jiggers Dry Gin
1 Jigger Kirsch
3 Jiggers Grapefruit Juice
4 Jiggers White Wine

Shake well with ice and strain into glasses. Serve with twist of Lemon Peel.

Moonshine (for 6)

5 Jiggers Dry Gin
1-1/2 Jiggers Dry Vermouth
2 Jiggers Maraschino
1–2 Drops Pernod

Shake well with ice and strain into glass.

Moulin Rouge

1/2 Orange Gin
1/2 Apricot Brandy
3 Dashes Grenadine

Stir well with ice and strain into glass.

Mule Hind Leg

1/5 Dry Gin
1/5 Applejack
1/5 Benedictine
1/5 Maple Syrup
1/5 Apricot Brandy

Stir well with ice and strain into glass.

My Cocktail (same as Marny)

Napoleon

2 Jiggers Dry Gin
1 Dash Dubonnet

1 Dash Curaçao
1 Dash Fernet Branca

Stir well with ice and strain into glass. Squeeze Lemon Peel over top.

Newbury

1/2 Dry Gin
1/2 Sweet Vermouth
3 Dashes Curaçao
1 Twist Lemon Peel
1 Twist Orange Peel

Stir well with ice and strain into glass.

Nightmare

1/3 Dry Gin
1/3 Dubonnet
1/6 Cherry Brandy
1/6 Orange Juice

Shake well with ice and strain into glass.

Nineteen

1/3 Dry Gin
1/3 Kirsch
1/3 Dry Vermouth
4 Dashes Sugar Syrup
1 Dash Bitters

Stir well with ice and strain into glass. Serve with Cherry.

Nineteen-Twenty

2/3 Dry Gin
1/6 Dry Vermouth
1/6 Kirsch
1 Dash Orange Bitters
1 Teaspoon Groseille Syrup

Shake well with ice and strain into glass.

Noon

Prepare same as BRONX, adding white of 1 Egg.

No. 6

1 Jigger Dry Gin
1/2 Jigger Sweet Vermouth
1 Twist Orange Peel
1 Twist Lemon Peel
3 Dashes Curaçao

Shake well with ice and strain into glass. Serve with a Cherry.

Old Etonian

1/2 Dry Gin
1/2 Lillet
2 Dashes Orange Bitters
2 Dashes Crème de Noyau

Stir well with ice and strain into glass. Serve with twist of Orange Peel.

Old-Fashioned (with Gin)

1–2 Jiggers Dry Gin
1 Slice Lemon Peel
1/2 Piece Lump Sugar
1 Dash Angostura Bitters

Place Sugar in bottom of Old-Fashioned glass and sprinkle with Bitters. Add Lemon and ice cubes and fill with Gin as desired. Stir and serve.

Olivette

1-1/2 Jiggers English Gin
2 Dashes Sugar Syrup
2 Dashes Orange Bitters

Stir with ice and strain into glass. Serve with twist of Lemon Peel, and an Olive if desired.

One Exciting Night

1/3 English Gin
1/3 Dry Vermouth
1/3 Sweet Vermouth
1 Dash Orange Juice

Shake well with ice and strain into glass. Twist Lemon Peel over top. Glasses should be frosted with Powdered Sugar.

One of Mine

1/2 Dry Gin
1/4 Dry Vermouth
1/4 Sweet Vermouth
Juice of 1/4 Orange
1 Dash Bitters

Stir well with ice and strain into glass.

Opal

1/2 Dry Gin
1/3 Orange Juice
1/6 Cointreau
1/4 Teaspoon Powdered Sugar

Shake well with ice and strain into glass. A little Orange Flower Water may be added, if available.

Opera

2/3 Dry Gin
1/6 Dubonnet
1/6 Maraschino

Stir well with ice and strain into glass. Squeeze Orange Peel over top.

Orange (for 6)

6 Jiggers Gin
3 Jiggers Orange Juice
1 Jigger Dry Vermouth
2 Dashes Orange Bitters
2 Teaspoons Powdered Sugar

Combine in shaker and place on ice for half an hour. Then shake with ice and strain into glasses. Serve with twists of Orange Peel.

Orange Bloom

1/2 Dry Gin
1/4 Sweet Vermouth
1/4 Cointreau

Stir with ice and strain into glass. Serve with a Cherry.

Orange Blossom

2–3 Jiggers Dry Gin
1 Jigger Orange Juice

Stir well with cracked ice and strain into glass. Powdered Sugar or Sugar Syrup may be added if desired.

Orange Martini (for 6)

5 Jiggers Gin
3 Jiggers Dry Vermouth
2 Jiggers Sweet Vermouth
1 Orange Rind, grated carefully

Steep the Orange Rind for two hours in the combined liquors. Shake well with ice and strain into glasses in each of which has been put a dash of Orange Bitters.

Pall Mall

1/3 English Gin
1/3 Dry Vermouth
1/3 Sweet Vermouth
1 Teaspoon White Crème de Menthe
1 Dash Orange Bitters

Stir well with ice and strain.

Paradise

1/3 Dry Gin
1/3 Apricot Brandy
1/3 Orange or Lemon Juice

Stir well with ice and strain.

Parisian

1/3 Dry Gin
1/3 Dry Vermouth
1/3 Crème de Cassis

Stir well with ice and strain.

Pat's Special (for 6)

4 Jiggers Dry Gin
4 Jiggers Sherry
4 Jiggers Quinquina
2 Dashes Crème de Cassis
2 Dashes Apricot Brandy

Shake well with ice and strain into glasses. Serve with Cherry and a piece of Orange Peel in each.

Peggy

2/3 Dry Gin
1/3 Dry Vermouth
1 Dash Pernod
1 Dash Dubonnet

Stir well with ice and strain into glass.

Pegu Club

2/3 Dry Gin
1/3 Curaçao
1 Dash Orange Bitters
1 Dash Angostura Bitters
1 Teaspoon Lime Juice

Shake well with ice and strain into glass.

Perfect

1/3 Dry Gin
1/3 Dry Vermouth
1/3 Sweet Vermouth

Stir well with ice and strain into glass.

Peter Pan

1/4 Dry Gin
1/4 Dry Vermouth
1/4 Orange Juice
1/4 Peach Brandy

Shake well with ice and strain into glass.

Peto

1/2 English Gin
1/4 Sweet Vermouth
1/4 Dry Vermouth
Juice of 1/4 Orange
2 Dashes Maraschino

Stir well with ice and strain into glass.

Piccadilly

2/3 Dry Gin
1/3 Dry Vermouth
1 Dash Pernod
1 Dash Grenadine

Stir well with ice and strain into glass.

Ping-Pong

1/2 Sloe Gin
1/2 Crème d'Yvette
Juice of 1/4 Lemon

Shake well with ice and strain into glass.

Ping-Pong Special (for 6)

5 Jiggers Sloe Gin
5 Jiggers Sweet Vermouth
1 Teaspoon Angostura Bitters
2 Teaspoons Curaçao

Stir well with ice and strain into glasses. Serve with a Cherry and a twist of Lemon Peel in each.

Pink Baby

1/2 Dry Gin
1/4 Grenadine
1/4 Sirop de Citron
1 Egg White

Shake well with ice and strain into glass.

Pink Gin (see Gin and Bitters)

Pink Lady No. 1

1 Jigger Dry Gin
1 Jigger Apple Brandy
1 Tablespoon Grenadine
1 Jigger Lemon Juice
1 Egg White

Shake well with ice and strain into glass.

Pink Lady No. 2

1 Jigger Gin
1/2 Jigger Lemon Juice
1 Tablespoon Grenadine
1 Egg White

Shake well and pour into chilled glass.

Pink Rose

2/3 Jigger Dry Gin
1 Teaspoon Grenadine
1 Teaspoon Lemon Juice
1 Teaspoon Cream
1 Egg White

Shake well with ice and strain into glass.

Pinky

1/2 Dry Gin
1/2 Grenadine
1 Egg White

Shake well with cracked ice and strain.

Plaza (see Hotel Plaza)

Pollyanna

1 Jigger Dry Gin
1/4 Jigger Grenadine
1/4 Jigger Sweet Vermouth
3 Slices Orange
3 Slices Pineapple

Muddle the Orange and Pineapple slices in the bottom of a shaker. Add ice and the other ingredients. Shake well and strain into glass.

Polo No. 1

1/3 Dry Gin
1/3 Dry Vermouth
1/3 Sweet Vermouth
Juice of 1/3 Lime

Shake well with ice and strain into glass.

Polo No. 2

2/3 English Gin
1/6 Grapefruit Juice
1/6 Orange Juice

Shake well with ice and strain into glass.

Polly or Poppy

2/3 Dry Gin
1/3 Crème de Cacao

Stir well with ice and strain into glass.

Pooh-Bah

1/3 Dry Gin
1/3 Light Rum
1/3 Swedish Punch
1 Dash Apricot Brandy

Stir well with ice and strain into glass.

Princess Mary

1/3 Dry Gin
1/3 Crème de Cacao
1/3 Cream

Shake well with ice and strain into glass.

Prince's Smile

1/2 Dry Gin
1/4 Calvados or Apple Brandy
1/4 Apricot Brandy
1 Dash Lemon Juice

Stir well with ice and strain into glass.

Princeton

1 Jigger Dry Gin
1/3 Jigger Port
2 Dashes Orange Bitters

Stir with ice and strain into glass. Serve with a twist of Lemon Peel.

Prohibition

1/2 Gin
1/2 Lillet
2 Dashes Orange Juice
1 Dash Apricot Brandy

Shake well with ice and strain into glass. Squeeze Lemon Peel over top.

Pruneaux (for 6)

4 Jiggers Gin
4 Jiggers Sherry

2 Jiggers Prune Syrup
2 Jiggers Orange Juice, strained

Shake thoroughly with cracked ice and strain into glasses.

Queen

2/3 Dry Gin
1/3 Sweet Vermouth
3 Slices Pineapple

Muddle Pineapple slices in shaker. Add other ingredients with ice. Stir well and strain into glass.

Queen Elizabeth

1/2 Dry Gin
1/4 Cointreau
1/4 Lemon Juice
1 Dash Pernod

Stir well with ice and strain into glass.

Queen's

1/2 Dry Gin
1/4 Dry Vermouth
1/4 Sweet Vermouth
1/2 Slice Pineapple

Muddle the Pineapple in shaker. Add ice and other ingredients and stir. Strain into glass.

R.A.C. Special

1/2 Dry Gin
1/4 Sweet Vermouth
1/4 Dry Vermouth
2 Dashes Orange Bitters

Stir well with ice and strain into glass. Squeeze Orange Peel over top.

Racquet Club

2/3 English Gin
1/3 Dry Vermouth
1 Dash Orange Bitters

Stir well with ice and strain into glass.

Raspberry (for 6)

4 Jiggers Dry Gin
1 Jigger Kirsch
4 Jiggers Dry White Wine
1 Cup Bruised Fresh Raspberries

Soak the Raspberries in the Gin for 2 hours. Strain and add other ingredients. Shake well with ice and strain into glasses. Serve with a fresh Raspberry in each.

Resolute

1/2 Dry Gin
1/4 Apricot Brandy
1/4 Lemon Juice

Stir well with ice and strain into glass.

Retreat from Moscow

1/2 Dry Gin
1/4 Kümmel
1/4 Lemon Juice

Shake well with ice and strain into glass.

Richmond

2/3 English Gin
1/3 Lillet

Stir well with ice and strain into glass. Squeeze Lemon Peel over top.

Riveredge (for 4 to 6)

4-1/2 Jiggers Dry Gin
1 Jigger Dry Vermouth
1/2 Jigger Water
4 Inch-wide Strips Orange Peel

Place all the ingredients, including the peel, in an electric mixer, and mix for two minutes. Strain into glasses and serve with a sliver of Orange Peel in each.

Roc-A-Coe

1/2 Dry Gin
1/2 Sherry

Stir well with ice and strain into glass. Serve with a Cherry.

Rolls Royce

1/2 Dry Gin
1/4 Dry Vermouth
1/4 Sweet Vermouth
1 or 2 Dashes Benedictine

Stir well with ice and strain into glass.

Rosa

1 Jigger Dry Gin
1/3 Jigger Kirsch
1/3 Jigger Apricot Brandy

Stir well with ice and strain into glass.

Rose (English) No. 1

1/2 Dry Gin
1/4 Dry Vermouth
1/4 Apricot Brandy
4 Dashes Grenadine
1 Dash Lemon Juice

Shake well with ice and strain into glass. Frost rim of glass with Powdered Sugar.

Rose (French) No. 2

1/2 Dry Gin
1/4 Dry Vermouth
1/4 Cherry Brandy

Stir well with ice and strain into glass. (Kirsch may be used instead of the Dry Vermouth.)

Roselyn

2/3 Dry Gin
1/3 Dry Vermouth
2 Dashes Grenadine

Stir well with ice and strain into glass. Squeeze Lemon Peel over top.

Rosington

2/3 Dry Gin
1/3 Sweet Vermouth

Stir well with ice and strain into glass. Squeeze Orange Peel over top.

Royal No. 1

1 Jigger Gin
Juice of 1/2 Lemon
1 Egg
1/2 Teaspoon Powdered Sugar

Shake well with ice and strain into glass.

Royal No. 2

1/3 Dry Gin
1/3 Dry Vermouth
1/3 Cherry Brandy

Stir well with ice and strain.

Royal No. 3

Prepare same as Royal No. 2, adding 1 dash Maraschino. Serve with a Cherry.

Royal Clover Club

2 Jiggers Gin
Juice of 1/2 Lemon
1 Tablespoon Grenadine
1 Egg Yolk

Shake well with ice and strain into glass.

Royal Smile

1/2 Dry Gin
1/2 Grenadine
2 Dashes Lemon Juice

Stir well with ice and strain into glass.

Russian

1/3 Dry Gin
1/3 Vodka
1/3 Crème de Cacao

Stir well with ice and strain into glass.

St. Mark

1/3 Burrough's Beefeater Gin
1/3 Dry Vermouth
1/6 Cherry Brandy
1/6 Groseille Syrup

Stir well with ice and strain into glass.

Salome

1/3 Dry Gin
1/3 Dry Vermouth
1/3 Dubonnet

Stir well with ice and strain into glass.

Sandmartin

1/2 Dry Gin
1/2 Sweet Vermouth
1 Teaspoon Green Chartreuse

Stir well with ice and strain into glass.

Sangaree

Prepare like BRONX, adding 1/4 jigger Crème de Rose, 1 twist Lemon Peel and white of 1 Egg.

Satan's Whiskers—Straight

1/5 Dry Gin
1/5 Dry Vermouth
1/5 Sweet Vermouth
1/5 Orange Juice
1/10 Grand Marnier
1/10 Orange Bitters

Stir well with ice and strain into glass.

Satan's Whiskers—Curled

Substitute Curaçao for the Grand Marnier in the foregoing recipe.

Savoy Hotel Special No. 1

2/3 Dry Gin
1/3 Dry Vermouth
2 Dashes Grenadine
1 Dash Pernod

Stir well with ice and strain into glass. Squeeze Lemon Peel over top.

Savoy Hotel Special No. 2

2/3 English Gin
1/3 Dry Vermouth
2 Dashes Dubonnet

Stir well with ice and strain into glass. Squeeze Orange Peel over top.

Savoy Tango

1/2 Sloe Gin
1/2 Applejack or Calvados

Shake well with ice and strain into glass.

Self-Starter

1/2 Dry Gin
3/8 Lillet
1/8 Apricot Brandy
2 Dashes Pernod

Stir well with ice and strain into glass.

Sensation

3/4 Dry Gin
1/4 Lemon Juice
3 Dashes Maraschino
3 Sprigs Fresh Mint

Shake well with ice and strain into glass.

Seventh Heaven No. 1

1/2 Dry Gin
1/2 Dubonnet
2 Dashes Maraschino
1 Dash Angostura Bitters

Stir well with ice and strain into glass. Squeeze Orange Peel on top. Serve with a Cherry.

Seventh Heaven No. 2

3/4 Dry Gin
1/4 Maraschino
1 Tablespoon Grapefruit Juice

Stir well with ice and strain into glass. Serve with a sprig of fresh Mint.

Seventh Regiment

2/3 Dry Gin
1/3 Sweet Vermouth
2 Twists of Thin Lemon Peel

Stir well with ice and strain into glass.

Shriner

1/2 Jigger Sloe Gin
1/2 Jigger Brandy
2 Dashes Sugar Syrup
2 Dashes Peychaud's Bitters

Stir well with ice and strain into glass. Serve with a twist of Lemon Peel.

Silver

1/2 Dry Gin
1/2 Dry Vermouth
2 Dashes Orange Bitters
2 Dashes Maraschino

Stir well with ice and strain into glass. Serve with twist of Lemon Peel.

Silver Bullet

1/2 Dry Gin
1/4 Kümmel
1/4 Lemon Juice

Stir well with ice and strain into glass.

Silver King

1 Jigger Dry Gin
Juice of 1/2 Lemon
2 Dashes Orange Bitters
2 Dashes Sugar Syrup
1 Egg White

Shake well with ice and strain into glass.

Silver Stallion

1/2 Dry Gin
1/2 Vanilla Ice Cream
Juice of 1/2 Lime
Juice of 1/2 Lemon

Shake with small amount of shaved ice. Strain into glass and fill with Soda Water.

Silver Streak

1/2 Dry Gin
1/2 Kümmel

Stir well with ice and strain into glass.

Sloeberry

2 Jiggers Sloe Gin
1 Dash Orange Bitters
1 Dash Angostura Bitters

Stir well with ice and strain into glass.

Sloe Gin

1 Jigger Sloe Gin
1 Dash Orange Bitters
1 Dash Dry Vermouth

Stir well with ice and strain into glass.

Smiler

1/2 Dry Gin
1/4 Dry Vermouth
1/4 Sweet Vermouth
1 Dash Angostura Bitters
1 Dash Orange Bitters

Stir well with ice and strain into glass.

Snapper **(see Gin Stinger)**

Snicker

2/3 Dry Gin
1/3 Dry Vermouth
2 Dashes Maraschino
1 Dash Orange Bitters
1 Teaspoon Sugar Syrup
1 Egg White

Shake well with ice and strain into glass.

Snowball

1/2 Dry Gin
1/8 Crème de Violette
1/8 White Crème de Menthe
1/8 Anisette
1/8 Cream

Shake well with ice and strain into glass.

Snyder

2 Dashes Curaçao
2/3 Dry Gin
1/3 Dry Vermouth

Stir well with ice and strain into glass. Serve with ice cube and twist of Orange Peel.

Some Moth

2/3 English Gin
1/3 Dry Vermouth
2 Dashes Pernod

Shake well with ice and strain into glass. Serve with a Pickled Pearl Onion.

Sonza's Wilson

1/2 Gin
1/2 Cherry Brandy
4 Dashes of Lemon or Lime Juice
4 Dashes Grenadine

Stir well with ice and strain into glass.

So-So

1/3 Dry Gin
1/3 Sweet Vermouth
1/6 Calvados or Apple Brandy
1/6 Grenadine

Stir well with ice and strain into glass.

Sour Kisses

2/3 Dry Gin
1/3 Dry Vermouth
1 Egg White

Shake well with ice and strain into glass.

Southern Bride

2/3 Dry Gin
1/3 Grapefruit Juice
3 Dashes Maraschino

Shake well with ice and strain into glass.

Southern Gin

2 Jiggers Dry Gin
2 Dashes Orange Bitters
2 Dashes Curaçao

Shake well with ice and strain into glass. Serve with a twist of Lemon Peel.

South Side

2 Jiggers Dry Gin
Juice of 1/2 Lemon
1/2 Tablespoon Powdered Sugar
2 Sprigs of Fresh Mint

Shake well with ice and

strain into glass. Add a dash of Soda Water if desired.

Spencer

2/3 Dry Gin
1/3 Apricot Brandy
1 Dash Orange Juice
1 Dash Angostura Bitters

Stir well with ice and strain into glass. Squeeze Orange Peel over top and serve with a Cherry.

Spring (for 6)

6 Jiggers Dry Gin
2 Jiggers Quinquina
2 Jiggers Benedictine
1 Dash Bitters

Shake well with ice and strain into glass. Serve with an Olive.

Spring Feeling

1/2 English Gin
1/4 Green Chartreuse
1/4 Lemon Juice

Stir well with ice and strain into glass.

Stanley

1/3 Gin
1/3 Rum
1/6 Grenadine
1/6 Lemon Juice

Stir well with ice and strain into glass.

Star No. 2

1/2 Dry Gin
1/2 Calvados or Apple Brandy
1 Dash Dry Vermouth
1 Dash Sweet Vermouth
1 Teaspoon Grapefruit Juice

Stir well with ice and strain into glass.

Straight Law

1/3 Dry Gin
2/3 Dry Sherry

Shake well with ice and strain into glass.

Strike's Off

1/2 Gin
1/4 Swedish Punch
1/4 Lemon Juice

Stir well with ice and strain into glass.

Submarine

1/2 Dry Gin
1/4 Dubonnet
1/4 Dry Vermouth
1 Dash Bitters

Stir well with ice and strain.

Summer Time

3/4 Gin
1/4 Sirop de Citron

Stir well with ice and strain into glass. Fill up with Soda Water.

Sunset (for 6)

Soak for 2 hours:

2 Jiggers Brandy
Rind of 1 Orange, slivered thin
1 Teaspoon Peach Preserve
1 Sliced Apricot with its crushed Kernel

Then add:

3 Jiggers Dry Gin
3 Jiggers White Wine
1 Jigger Dry Vermouth

Shake well with ice and strain into glass.

Sunshine No. 1

2/3 Dry Gin
1/3 Sweet Vermouth
1 Dash Angostura Bitters
1 Lump of Ice

Stir together and strain into glass. Squeeze Orange Peel over top.

Sweet Patootie

1/2 Dry Gin
1/4 Cointreau
1/4 Orange Juice

Stir well with ice and strain into glass.

Swizzles

2 Jiggers Gin
Juice of 1 Lime
1 Dash Angostura Bitters
1 Teaspoon Sugar

Stir with swizzle stick until it foams. Add 1 lump of Ice.

Tango

1/2 Dry Gin
1/4 Sweet Vermouth
1/4 Dry Vermouth
2 Dashes Curaçao
Juice of 1/4 Orange

Stir well with ice and strain into glass.

Third Degree

2/3 English Gin
1/3 Dry Vermouth
4 Dashes Pernod

Stir well with ice and strain into glass.

Three Stripes

2/3 Dry Gin
1/3 Dry Vermouth
3 Slices Orange

Shake well with ice and strain into glass.

Thunderclap

1/3 Gin
1/3 Whiskey
1/3 Brandy

Shake well with ice and strain into glass. Drink this at your own risk!

Tidbit

1/2 Dry Gin
1/2 Vanilla Ice Cream
1 Dash Sherry

Shake well till thoroughly blended. If you think anything else is necessary, serve with a Cherry.

Tipperary No. 1

1/3 Dry Gin
1/3 Dry Vermouth
1/6 Orange Juice
1/6 Grenadine
2 Sprigs of Mint

Shake well with ice and strain into glass.

Transvaal

1/2 Gin
1/2 Dubonnet
3 Dashes Orange Bitters

Stir well with ice and strain into glass.

Trilby No. 1

1/2 Gin
1/2 Sweet Vermouth
2 Dashes Orange Bitters

Shake well with ice and strain into a glass. Float a little Crème d'Yvette on top and serve.

Trinity

1/3 Dry Gin
1/3 Dry Vermouth
1/3 Sweet Vermouth

Stir well with ice and strain into glass.

Turf or Tuxedo No. 1

1/2 Gin
1/2 Dry Vermouth
2 Dashes Pernod
1 Piece Lemon Peel

Stir well with ice and strain into glass.

Tuxedo No. 2

1/2 Dry Gin
1/2 Dry Vermouth
2 Dashes Orange Bitters
1 Dash Pernod
1 Dash Maraschino

Stir well with ice and strain into glass. Add a Cherry and squeeze Lemon Peel over the top.

Twin Six

1 Jigger Gin
1/2 Jigger Sweet Vermouth
1 Dash Grenadine
3 Slices Orange
1 Egg White

Shake well with ice and strain into glass.

Ulanda

2/3 Dry Gin
1/3 Cointreau
1 Dash Pernod

Stir well with ice and strain into glass.

Union Jack

2/3 Dry Gin
1/3 Crème d'Yvette

Stir well with ice and strain into glass.

Up in the Air

1 Jigger Dry Gin
1/3 Jigger Lemon Juice
2 Teaspoons Maraschino

Shake well with ice and strain into glass. If you go for such fancies, a dash of Blue Vegetable Extract may be added.

Van

2/3 Dry Gin
1/3 Dry Vermouth
2 Dashes Grand Marnier

Stir well with ice and strain into glass.

Velocity

1/3 Dry Gin
2/3 Sweet Vermouth
1 Slice Orange

Shake well with ice and strain into glass.

Victor

1/4 Dry Gin
1/4 Brandy
1/2 Sweet Vermouth

Stir well with ice and strain into glass.

Vie Rose

1/3 Dry Gin
1/3 Kirsch
1/6 Lemon Juice
1/6 Grenadine

Shake well with ice and strain into glass.

Virgin

1/3 Dry Gin
1/3 Forbidden Fruit Liqueur
1/3 White Crème de Menthe

Stir well with ice and strain into glass.

Waldorf

1/4 Dry Gin
1/2 Swedish Punch
Juice of 1/4 Lemon or Lime

Shake well with ice and strain into glass.

Wallick

1/2 Dry Gin
1/2 Dry Vermouth
3 Dashes Orange Flower Water

Stir well with ice and strain into glass. Curaçao may be used in place of the Orange Flower Water.

Wardays

1/3 Dry Gin
1/3 Sweet Vermouth
1/3 Calvados or Apple Brandy
1 Teaspoon Yellow Chartreuse

Shake well with ice and strain into glass.

Ward Eight No. 1

Prepare same as MARTINI (dry), adding 2 twists of Orange Peel.

Wax

2 Jiggers English Gin
3 Dashes Orange Bitters

Stir well with ice and strain into glass.

Webster

1/2 English Gin
1/4 Dry Vermouth
1/8 Apricot Brandy
1/8 Lime Juice

Shake well with ice and strain into glass.

Wedding Belle

1/3 Dry Gin
1/3 Dubonnet

1/6 Orange Juice
1/6 Cherry Brandy

Shake well with ice and strain into glass.

Weesuer Special

1/4 Dry Gin
1/4 Curaçao
1/4 Dry Vermouth
1/4 Sweet Vermouth
4 Dashes Pernod

Stir well with ice and strain into glass.

Welcome Stranger

1/6 Dry Gin
1/6 Swedish Punch
1/6 Brandy
1/6 Grenadine
1/6 Lemon Juice
1/6 Orange Juice

Shake well with ice and strain into glass.

Wellington

1 Jigger Dry Gin
2 Dashes Swedish Punch
2 Dashes Cherry Brandy
Juice of 1/2 Lime

Stir well with ice and strain into glass.

Wembley No. 1

2/3 Dry Gin
1/3 Dry Vermouth
2–3 Dashes Calvados or Apple Brandy

Stir well with ice and strain into glass.

Westbrook (for 6)

5 Jiggers Dry Gin
2 Jiggers Sweet Vermouth
2 Jiggers Bourbon Whiskey
1/2 Teaspoon Powdered Sugar

Shake well with ice and strain into glass.

Western Rose

1/2 Dry Gin
1/4 Dry Vermouth
1/4 Apricot Brandy
1 Dash Lemon Juice

Stir well with ice and strain into glass.

West Indian

2 Jiggers Burrough's Beefeater Gin
4 Dashes Angostura Bitters
1 Teaspoon Sugar
1 Teaspoon Lemon Juice
2 Cubes Ice

Combine, stir and serve in the same glass.

White

2 Jiggers Dry Gin
2 Teaspoons Anisette
2 Dashes Orange Bitters

Stir well with ice and strain into glass. Squeeze Lemon Peel over top.

White Baby

1/2 Dry Gin
1/4 Cointreau
1/4 Sirop de Citron

Stir well with ice and strain into glass.

White Cargo

1/2 Dry Gin
1/2 Vanilla Ice Cream

No ice is necessary. Shake together till blended and pour into glass.

White Lady

1/2 Dry Gin
1/4 Cointreau
1/4 Lemon Juice

Shake well with ice and strain into glass.

White Lily

1/3 Dry Gin
1/3 Light Rum
1/3 Cointreau
1 Dash Pernod

Stir well with ice and strain into glass.

White Plush

2 Jiggers Dry Gin
2/3 Jigger Maraschino
1 Cup Milk

Shake well with ice and strain into glass.

White Rose

1 Jigger Dry Gin
Juice of 1/4 Orange
Juice of 1 Lime
1/2 Jigger Maraschino
1 Egg White

Shake well with ice and strain into glass.

White Way No. 2

2/3 Dry Gin
1/3 White Crème de Menthe

Shake well with ice and strain into glass. This is similar to the GIN STINGER.

White Wings (same as White Way)

Whizz-Doodle

1/4 Dry Gin
1/4 Crème de Cacao
1/4 Scotch Whisky
1/4 Cream

Shake well with ice and strain into glass.

Why Not

1/3 Dry Gin
1/3 Dry Vermouth
1/2 Apricot Brandy
1 Dash Lemon Juice

Shake well with ice and strain into glass.

Wild Oat

3/4 Dry Gin
1/4 Kirsch
1 Dash Lemon Juice
1 Dash Apricot Brandy

Shake well with ice and strain into glass.

Will Rogers

1/2 English Gin
1/4 Dry Vermouth
1/4 Orange Juice
4 Dashes Curaçao

Shake well with ice and strain into glass.

Wilson Special

2 Jiggers Dry Gin
2 Dashes Dry Vermouth
2 Slices Orange or Blood Orange, if available

Shake well with ice and strain into glass.

Xanthia

1/3 Dry Gin
1/3 Yellow Chartreuse
1/3 Cherry Brandy

Stir well with ice and strain into glass.

Yachting Club

2/3 Holland Gin
1/3 Dry Vermouth
2 Dashes Sugar Syrup
2 Dashes Peychaud's Bitters
1 Dash Pernod

Stir well with ice and strain into glass.

Yale

1 Jigger Dry Gin
1/2 Jigger Dry Vermouth
3 Dashes Orange Bitters
2 Dashes Sugar Syrup
1 Dash Maraschino

Stir well with ice and strain into glass.

Yellow Daisy (for 6)

4 Jiggers Dry Gin
4 Jiggers Dry Vermouth
2 Jiggers Grand Marnier
1 Dash Pernod

Shake well with ice and strain into glasses. Serve with a Cherry.

Yellow Rattler

1/4 Dry Gin
1/4 Dry Vermouth
1/4 Sweet Vermouth
1/4 Orange Juice

Shake well with ice and strain into glass with small crushed pickled Onion.

Yokohama

1/3 Dry Gin
1/6 Vodka
1/3 Orange Juice
1/6 Grenadine
1 Dash Pernod

Stir well with ice and strain into glass.

Yolanda

1/4 Dry Gin
1/4 Brandy
1/2 Sweet Vermouth
1 Dash Grenadine
1 Dash Pernod

Stir well with ice and strain into glass.

Zaza

1 Jigger Dry Gin
1 Jigger Dubonnet
1 Twist Orange Peel

Stir well with ice and strain into glass.

LIQUEUR BASES

Many of the following cocktails call for equal quantities of Liqueurs. Hence their listing has been arbitrary.

APRICOT BRANDY

After Dinner

1/2 Apricot Brandy
1/2 Curaçao
Juice of 1 Lime, with twist of Peel

Shake well with ice and strain into glass.

After Supper

1/2 Apricot Brandy
1/2 Curaçao
2 Dashes Lemon Juice

Stir well with ice and strain into glass.

Apricot

1/2 Apricot Brandy
1/4 Orange Juice
1/4 Lemon Juice
1 Dash Dry Gin

Shake well with ice and strain into glass.

Babbie's Special

2/3 Apricot Brandy
1/3 Cream
1 Dash Gin

Shake well with ice and strain into glass.

Culross

1/3 Apricot Brandy
1/3 Light Rum
1/3 Lillet
Juice of 1/4 Lemon

Stir well with ice and strain into glass.

Ethel Duffy

1/3 Apricot Brandy
1/3 White Crème de Menthe
1/3 Curaçao

Shake well with ice and strain into glass.

Festival

1/2 Jigger Apricot Brandy
1/2 Jigger Crème de Cacao
1/2 Jigger Cream
1 Teaspoon Grenadine

Shake well with ice and strain into large cocktail glass.

Flag

Place a teaspoon of Crème d'Yvette in a cocktail glass. Shake with shaved ice 1 jigger Apricot Brandy and 4 dashes Curaçao. Pour into glass carefully so as not to mix. Top with Claret.

Havana No. 1

1/2 Apricot Brandy
1/4 Swedish Punch
1/4 Dry Gin
1 Dash Lemon Juice

Stir well with ice and strain into glass.

Hop Toad

3/4 Apricot Brandy
1/4 Lemon Juice

Stir well with ice and strain into glass.

Mother Sherman

1-1/2 Jiggers Apricot Brandy
2/3 Jigger Orange Juice
4 Dashes Orange Bitters

Shake well with shaved ice and strain into large cocktail glass.

Princess

3/4 Apricot Brandy
1/4 Cream

Pour Brandy into cocktail glass and top with Cream so they do not mix. Serve after dinner.

Tempter

1/2 Apricot Brandy
1/2 Port

Stir well with ice and strain into glass.

Tender

1/4 Apricot Brandy
1/4 Apple Brandy
1/2 Gin
1 Dash Lemon Juice

Shake well with ice and strain into glass.

Valencia

2/3 Apricot Brandy
1/3 Orange Juice
4 Dashes Orange Bitters

Stir well with ice and strain into glass. This may also be poured into a tall glass and filled with Champagne.

Yellow Parrot

1/3 Apricot Brandy
1/3 Yellow Chartreuse
1/3 Pernod

Shake well with ice and strain into glass.

BENEDICTINE

B. and B.

1/2 Benedictine
1/2 Brandy

Serve in a liqueur glass or iced in a cocktail glass. This is an after-dinner drink.

Benedictine

Place in a shaker with ice 2 jiggers Benedictine and a dash of Angostura Bitters. Shake slightly and strain into a cocktail glass, the rim of which has been rubbed with a slice of Lemon and then dipped into Powdered Sugar. Serve with a Maraschino Cherry.

Benedictine Cocktail

Rub the rim of a cocktail glass with Lemon and dip in Powdered Sugar. Place a Cherry in and add the following mixture: Combine in a shaker, with ice, 1 dash Angostura Bitters and 1 jigger Benedictine. Shake slightly and strain into prepared glass.

Benedictine Frappé

Fill a large cocktail glass with shaved ice and fill with Benedictine. Serve after dinner with straws.

Widow's Dream

2 Jiggers Benedictine
1 Egg
1 Jigger Cream

Shake well with ice and strain into glass.

BLACKBERRY

Windy Corner

2 Jiggers Blackberry
Brandy

Shake well with shaved ice and serve with a grating of Nutmeg.

You Never Know

2 Jiggers Blackberry Brandy
1 Jigger White Crème de Menthe
1 Grating of Nutmeg

Stir well with ice and strain into glass.

CHARTREUSE

Chocolate No. 2

1 Jigger Yellow Chartreuse
1 Jigger Maraschino
1 Egg
1 Teaspoon Powdered Sugar

Shake well with ice and strain into glass.

Golden Slipper

1/2 Jigger Yellow Chartreuse
1/2 Jigger Eau de Vie Danzig
1 Egg Yolk

Shake well with ice and strain into glass.

Green Dragon No. 2

1/2 Green Chartreuse
1/2 Brandy

Stir with shaved ice and strain into glass.

H-Bomb

1/4 Yellow Chartreuse
1/4 Green Chartreuse
1/4 Brandy
1/4 Bourbon Whiskey

Shake well with ice and strain into glass.

Rainbow

1/7 Yellow Chartreuse
1/7 Green Chartreuse
1/7 Crème de Cacao
1/7 Crème de Violette
1/7 Maraschino
1/7 Benedictine
1/7 Brandy

Pour ingredients carefully into large liqueur glass so that they do not mix. Serve only after dinner.

St. Germain

2 Jiggers Green Chartreuse
1 Egg White
Juice of 1/2 Lemon or 1/4 Grapefruit

Shake well with ice and strain into glass.

Stars and Stripes

1/3 Green Chartreuse
1/3 Maraschino
1/3 Crème de Cassis

Pour carefully into liqueur glass so that ingredients do not mix. Serve after dinner.

Union Jack

1/3 Green Chartreuse
1/3 Maraschino
1/3 Grenadine

Pour ingredients carefully into liqueur glass so that they do not mix. Serve after dinner.

CHERRY BRANDY

Bulldog

1 Jigger Cherry Brandy
1/2 Light Rum
Juice of 1/2 Lime

Shake well with ice and strain into glass.

Merry Widow

1/2 Cherry Brandy
1/2 Maraschino

Shake well with ice and serve with a Cherry.

Purple Bunny

1 Jigger Cherry Brandy
1/3 Jigger Crème de Cacao
2/3 Jigger Cream

Shake well with ice and strain into large cocktail glass.

Wallick's

1/2 Cherry Brandy
1/2 White Curaçao

Shake well with ice and strain into glass.

COINTREAU

Albertine

1/3 Cointreau
1/3 Yellow Chartreuse
1/3 Kirsch
1 Dash Maraschino

Shake well with ice and strain into glass.

Blanche

1/3 Cointreau
1/3 Anisette
1/3 White Curaçao

Shake well with ice and strain into glass.

Broadway Smile

1/3 Cointreau
1/3 Swedish Punch
1/3 Crème de Cassis

Pour carefully into liqueur glass so that ingredients do not mix. Serve after dinner.

Bud's Special

2/3 Cointreau
1/3 Cream
1 Dash Angostura Bitters

Stir well with ice and strain into glass.

Lollypop (for 6)

2 Jiggers Cointreau
2 Jiggers Chartreuse
2 Jiggers Kirsch
1 Dash Maraschino

Shake well with ice and strain into glasses. Serve after dinner.

Sunrise

1/4 Cointreau
1/4 Yellow Chartreuse
1/4 Crème de Violette
1/4 Grenadine

Pour carefully into liqueur glass so that ingredients do not mix. Serve after dinner.

CRÈME DE CACAO

Angel's Kiss

1/4 Crème de Cacao
1/4 Prunelle
1/4 Crème de Violette
1/4 Sweet Cream

Pour ingredients carefully into glass so that they do not mix.

Angel's Tip

3/4 Crème de Cacao
1/4 Cream

Pour carefully into liqueur glass, floating Cream on top.

Angel's Wing

1/2 Crème de Cacao
1/2 Prunelle

Pour ingredients carefully into glass so that they do not mix and float Cream on top.

Golden Gopher

1 Jigger White Crème de Cacao
1 Jigger Brandy

Stir well with ice and strain into glass.

Layer Cake

1/3 Crème de Cacao
1/3 Apricot Brandy
1/3 Cream

Pour carefully into liqueur glass so that ingredients do not mix. Place Cherry on top. Chill mixture in glass.

Liebfraumilch

1 Jigger Crème de Cacao
1 Jigger Cream
Juice of 1 Lime

Shake well with ice and strain into glass.

Witching Eve

2/3 Crème de Cacao
1 Dash Angostura Bitters
1/3 Cream

Pour carefully into liqueur glass so that ingredients do not mix.

CRÈME DE MENTHE

Diana

3/4 White Crème de Menthe
Shaved Ice
1/4 Brandy

Place ice in glass and pour in Crème de Menthe. Top carefully with Brandy.

Frappé (Crème de Menthe)

Fill cocktail glass with shaved ice. Pour in Green or White Crème de Menthe.

Grasshopper

2/3 Jigger Green Crème de Menthe
2/3 Jigger White Crème de Cacao
2/3 Jigger Cream

Shake well with ice and serve in Champagne glass.

Pousse Café

1/6 Grenadine
1/6 Maraschino
1/6 Green Crème de Menthe
1/6 Crème de Violette
1/6 Chartreuse
1/6 Brandy

Add carefully in order given to keep each liqueur separate.

Stinger (see Brandy)

CRÈME DE VIOLETTE

Angel's Wings

1/3 Crème de Violette
1/3 Raspberry Syrup
1/3 Maraschino

Pour ingredients carefully into liqueur glass so that they do not mix.

CRÈME D'YVETTE

Lillian Waldorf

1/2 Jigger Crème d'Yvette
1/2 Jigger Maraschino

Pour carefully and top with Cream.

CURAÇAO

Baby's Own

2/3 White Curaçao
1/3 Cream
1 Dash Angostura Bitters

Shake well with ice and strain into glass.

Canadian No. 1

1 Jigger Curaçao
3 Dashes Jamaica Rum
1 Teaspoon Powdered Sugar
Juice of 1/2 Lemon

Shake well with ice and strain into glass.

Curaçao (for 6)

5 Jiggers Curaçao
5 Jiggers Orange Juice
1 Jigger Brandy
1 Jigger Dry Gin

Shake well with ice and strain into glasses rinsed with Orange Bitters.

Double Arrow

1/2 Light Curaçao
1/2 Crème d'Yvette
Cream

Pour carefully into liqueur glasses so that liqueurs do not mix, and top with Cream.

Five Fifteen

1/3 Curaçao
1/3 Dry Vermouth
1/3 Cream

Shake well with ice and strain into glass.

GRAND MARNIER

Alfonso Special

1/2 Grand Marnier
1/4 Dry Vermouth

1/4 Dry Gin
4 Dashes Sweet Vermouth
1 Dash Angostura Bitters

Stir well with ice and strain into glass.

Gloom Chaser

1/4 Grand Marnier
1/4 Curaçao
1/4 Lemon Juice
1/4 Grenadine

Stir well with ice and strain into glass.

Red Lion

2/3 Jigger Grand Marnier
2/3 Jigger Dry Gin
1/3 Jigger Lemon Juice
1/3 Jigger Orange Juice

Shake well with ice and strain into glass. Serve with twist of Lemon Peel.

KIRSCH

Café Kirsch

1 Jigger Kirsch
1 Teaspoon Sugar
2 Jiggers Cold Coffee
1 Egg White

Shake well with ice and strain into glass.

Rose No. 3

1/2 Kirsch
1/2 Dry Vermouth
1 Teaspoon Grenadine

Stir well with ice and strain into glass.

MARASCHINO

Knickerbein

1 Jigger Maraschino
1 Jigger Grenadine
1 Egg Yolk
1 Jigger Brandy

Shake well with ice and strain into glass.

SLOE GIN

Sloe Gin No. 1

1-1/2 Jiggers Sloe Gin
1/2 Jigger Dry Vermouth

Stir well with ice and strain into glass.

Sloe Gin No. 2

1-1/2 Jiggers Sloe Gin
2 Dashes Orange Bitters
2 Dashes Angostura Bitters

Shake well with ice and strain into glass.

Ninety Miles

1/2 Sloe Gin
1/2 Applejack

Shake well with ice and strain into glass.

Queen Bee

2/3 Sloe Gin
1/3 Curaçao
1 Dash Anisette

Shake well with ice and strain into glass.

White Man's Burden

1 Jigger Sloe Gin
1/3 Jigger Apricot Brandy
Juice of 1/2 Lime

Shake well with ice and strain into glass.

SOUTHERN COMFORT

Memphis Belle

Place 1/2 Peach and a Maraschino Cherry in a Champagne glass. Add shaved ice and fill with Southern Comfort. Serve with short straws and a small spoon.

Old-Fashioned

Put 1 dash Angostura Bitters in Old-Fashioned glass. Add a twist of Lemon Peel and ice cubes. Fill with Southern Comfort as desired.

Rhett Butler

1 Jigger Southern Comfort
Juice of 1/4 Lime
Juice of 1/4 Lemon
1 Teaspoon Curaçao
1/2 Teaspoon Powdered Sugar

Shake well with ice and strain into glass.

Scarlett O'Hara

1-1-2 Jiggers Southern Comfort
1-1/2 Cranberry Juice
Juice of 1/4 Lime

Stir well with ice and strain into glass.

COCKTAILS AND DRINKS

NON-ALCOHOLIC

Basic Tea Punch

2 Cups Strong Hot Tea
6 Cups Fruit Juice
1/4 Ginger Ale or Soda Water

Combine just before serving and sweeten to taste with Sugar or Syrup, etc. Pour over a block of ice in a punch bowl and chill.

Black Cow

Fill a tall glass 3/4 full of Sarsaparilla and add 1 or 2 scoops of Vanilla Ice Cream.

Black and Tan

Fill a tall glass, with 1 or 2 ice cubes, 2/3 full of Cola. Fill up with Milk. Stir and serve.

Clam Juice Cocktail

Combine in a shaker 1 teaspoon Tomato Catsup, 1 pinch Celery Salt, 1 or 2 dashes Tabasco Sauce and 2/3 cup Clam Juice. Shake well with 1 or 2 ice cubes and strain into small tumbler.

Clam Juice-Tomato Cocktail

Prepare same as CLAM JUICE COCKTAIL, omitting Catsup and using half and half Clam Juice and Tomato Juice.

Club Cocktail

1 Lump Sugar
2 Dashes Angostura Bitters
1 Long Twist Lemon Peel
Soda Water

Place Sugar in Old-Fashioned glass and splash with Bitters. Add other ingredients with ice cubes and fill with Soda Water.

Eggnog

1 Egg
1 Tablespoon Sugar
1 Pinch Salt
1/4 Teaspoon Vanilla
Milk

Beat Egg with Salt and Sugar. Pour into tall glass, add Vanilla and fill with Milk. Stir and sprinkle lightly with Nutmeg.

Grape Juice Cup (for 10)

Place ice cubes in a large pitcher and add the Juice of 6 Lemons, 1 quart of Grape Juice and fill with Soda Water. Add Grenadine to taste and decorate with fruit as desired. Stir and serve.

Lemonade (for 4 to 6)

Juice of 6 Lemons
1 Quart Water
1 Cup Sugar Syrup or other Sweetening

Combine in pitcher and chill. Pour over ice cubes in tall glasses. Garnish with fruit or Mint as desired.

Orangeade (for 4 to 6)

Juice of 5 Oranges
Juice of 1 Lemon
1/2 Cup Sugar Syrup
1 Quart Water

Prepare and serve same as LEMONADE.

Parisette

Place in a tumbler several ice cubes, 1 tablespoon Grenadine and fill with cold Milk. Stir and serve.

Pink Pearl (for 6)

1 Cup Grapefruit Juice
2 Teaspoons Lemon Juice
1 or 2 Tablespoons Grenadine
1 or 2 Egg Whites

Shake with crushed ice and strain into cocktail glasses.

Prairie Oyster No. 2

1 Egg Yolk
2 Dashes Vinegar
1 Teaspoon Worcestershire Sauce
1 Dash Tabasco Sauce
1 Pinch Salt

Slip Egg Yolk carefully into small glass. Add seasonings.

Rail Splitter

Juice of 1/2 Lemon
2/3 Jigger Sugar Syrup

Pour into glass with ice and fill up with Ginger Beer.

Rosey Squash

Place in a tumbler with ice cubes the Juice of 1/2 Lemon, 1 tablespoon Grenadine and fill up with Soda Water.

Saratoga No. 2

Juice of 1/2 Lemon
1/2 Teaspoon Powdered Sugar
2 Dashes Angostura Bitters
Ginger Ale

Place ingredients in tall glass with ice cubes and fill with Ginger Ale.

Sherbet Punch (for 12)

Place a large piece of ice in a punch bowl and add 1 pint Orange Sherbet and 1 quart Ginger Ale. Break the Sherbet into chunks and pour the Ginger Ale over it. Decorate with Mint Leaves and serve in punch cups.

Spiced Cider (for 4)

1 Quart Apple Cider
1/4 Cup Sugar
1/8 Teaspoon Salt
1 Cinnamon Stick, broken
12 Whole Cloves
8 Whole Allspice

Combine ingredients in a saucepan and bring to a boil. Cool and let stand for several hours. Strain and reheat before serving.

Spiced Lemonade

1 Cup Sugar Syrup
12 Whole Cloves
1 Stick Cinnamon
Juice of 6 Lemons
1 Quart Water

Cook Sugar, Cloves and Cinnamon for 5 minutes. Add Lemon Juice and let stand 1 hour. Add Water and strain into glasses over crushed ice.

Summer Delight

Place 2 or 3 ice cubes in a large tumbler. Add the Juice of 1 Lime and 1/2 Jigger Raspberry Syrup. Fill up with Soda Water and decorate with fruit as desired. Stir and serve.

Summer Fizz (for 8)

12 Sprigs Mint
1/2 Cup Lemon Juice
1 Cup Currant Jelly
1 Cup Hot Water
1 Cup Cold Water
3 Cups Orange Juice
1 Bottle Ginger Ale

Crush Mint in a bowl and add boiling Water and 1 cup Currant Jelly. When Jelly is melted, add cold Water. Strain when cold into punch bowl. Add Fruit Juices and block of ice. Just before serving, pour in Ginger Ale and decorate with Mint.

Temperance Cup (for 10)

Combine in punch bowl, with a block of ice, the Juice of 4 Oranges, the Juice of 1 Lemon, the Juice of 5 Limes, 3 tablespoons Powdered Sugar and 1 quart Grape Juice. Stir and decorate with fruit as desired.

Temperance Punch

1/2 Pound Powdered Sugar
1 Quart Cold Tea
1 Pint Lemon Juice
1 Quart Soda Water
2 Quarts White Grape Juice

Combine all ingredients in punch bowl with a block of ice. Stir and decorate with fruit as desired.

Tomato Juice Cocktail

Combine in shaker with ice 2/3 cup Tomato Juice, Juice of 1/4 Lemon, 1 pinch of Salt, 1 teaspoon Worcestershire Sauce. Shake well and strain into small tumbler.

RUM BASE

Apple Pie

1/2 Light Rum
1/2 Sweet Vermouth
4 Dashes Apricot Brandy
4 Dashes Lemon Juice
2 Dashes Grenadine

Shake well with ice and strain into glass.

Bacardi No. 1

2 Jiggers Bacardi Rum
Juice of 1/2 Lime
2 Dashes Sugar Syrup

Shake well with ice and strain into glass.

Bacardi No. 2

Prepare same as No. 1, substituting Grenadine for Sugar Syrup.

Bacardi Special

2/3 Light Rum
1/3 English Gin
Juice of 1/2 Lime
1 Teaspoon Grenadine

Shake well with ice and strain into glass.

Beachcomber

1-1/2 Jiggers Light Rum
1/2 Jigger Cointreau
Juice of 1/2 Lime
2 Dashes Maraschino

Shake with shaved ice and serve in large cocktail glass.

Bee's Kiss

1 Jigger Rum
1 Teaspoon Honey
1 Teaspoon Cream

Shake well with ice and strain into glass.

Bolo

2 Jiggers Light Rum
Juice of 1/2 Lemon or Lime
Juice of 1/4 Orange
1 Teaspoon Powdered Sugar

Shake well with ice and strain into glass.

Bushranger

1/2 Light Rum
1/2 Dubonnet
2 Dashes Angostura Bitters

Shake well with ice and strain into glass.

Chinese

2/3 Jamaica Rum
1/3 Grenadine
3 Dashes Curaçao
3 Dashes Maraschino
1 Dash Angostura Bitters

Stir well with ice and strain into glass. Serve with Cherry.

Clayton's Special

1/2 Light Rum
1/4 Cola
1/4 Sirop de Citron

Shake well with ice and strain into glass.

Columbia

1 Jigger Light Rum
1/3 Jigger Raspberry Syrup
1/3 Lemon Juice

Shake well with ice and strain into glass.

Country Life

1/2 Jigger Jamaica Rum
1/2 Jigger Port
1 Jigger Bourbon Whiskey
3 Dashes Angostura Bitters
1 Dash Orange Bitters

Shake well with ice and strain into glass.

Cuban No. 2 (see Bacardi No. 1)

Cuban No. 3

1-1/2 Bacardi Rum
1/2 Apricot Brandy
Juice of 1/2 Lime

Shake well with ice and strain into glass.

Cuban No. 4

1 Jigger Bacardi Rum
1 Jigger Pineapple Juice
1 Teaspoon Grenadine
1 Teaspoon Maraschino

Fill large glass with shaved ice and pour mixed ingredients over. Serve with straws.

Daiquiri

1-1/2 Jiggers Light Rum
Juice of 1/2 Lime

1 Teaspoon Powdered Sugar

Shake well with ice and strain into glass.

Daiquiri (frozen)

2 Jiggers Light Rum
1 Tablespoon Lime or Lemon Juice
2 Teaspoons Powdered Sugar

Place 2 cups shaved ice in a blender. Add ingredients and blend until consistency of snow. Serve immediately with straw. With a blender, fresh or frozen fruit or juices may be added to the DAIQUIRI, as desired.

Davis

1/2 Jamaica Rum
1/2 Dry Vermouth
2 Dashes Raspberry Syrup
Juice of 1 Lime

Shake well with ice and strain into glass.

Dunlop

2/3 Light Rum
1/3 Sherry
1 Dash Angostura Bitters

Stir well with ice and strain into glass.

El Presidente

1 Jigger Gold Label Rum
1/3 Jigger Curaçao
1/3 Jigger Dry Vermouth
1 Dash Grenadine

Shake well with ice and strain into glass.

Eyeopener

1 Jigger Light Rum
2 Dashes Crème de Noyau
2 Dashes Curaçao
2 Dashes Pernod
1 Teaspoon Powdered Sugar
1 Egg Yolk

Shake well with ice and strain into glass.

Fair and Warmer

2/3 Light Rum
1/3 Sweet Vermouth
2 Dashes Curaçao

Stir well with ice and strain into glass. Serve with twist of Lemon Peel.

Fireman's Sour

2 Jiggers Light Rum
1/2 Teaspoon Powdered Sugar
Juice of 1 Lime
1/3 Jigger Grenadine

Shake well with ice and strain into Delmonico glass. Decorate with fruit if desired.

Flanagan

1 Jigger Myers' Jamaica Rum
1 Jigger Sweet Vermouth
1/2 Teaspoon Sugar Syrup
1 Dash Angostura Bitters

Shake well with ice and strain into glass.

Florida Special No. 1

1 Jigger Puerto Rican Rum
1 Teaspoon Dry Vermouth
1 Teaspoon Sweet Vermouth
2/3 Jigger Unsweetened Grapefruit Juice

Stir with shaved ice and strain into glass.

Fluffy Ruffles

1/2 Light Rum
1/2 Sweet Vermouth
1 Twist of Lime or Lemon Peel

Stir well with ice and strain into glass.

Four Flush

1/2 Light Rum
1/4 Swedish Punch
1/4 Dry Vermouth
1 Dash Grenadine or Sugar Syrup

Stir well with ice and strain into glass.

Fox Trot

2 Jiggers Light Rum
2 Dashes Curaçao
Juice of 1/2 Lime or Lemon

Shake well with ice and strain into glass.

Full House

1/2 Bacardi Rum
1/4 Swedish Punch
1/4 Dry Vermouth

Stir well with ice and strain into glass.

Governor's

Before your cocktail party place 1 Vanilla Bean in a bottle of Martinique Rum and leave it 24 hours. For your drinks place 1 or 2 ice cubes in a Champagne glass with 1 teaspoon Sugar Syrup and 1 twist Lime Peel. Fill up with Rum.

Gradeal Special

1/2 Light Rum
1/4 Apricot Brandy
1/4 Dry Gin

Stir well with ice and strain into glass.

Havana No. 2

1 Jigger Light Rum
2/3 Jigger Pineapple Juice
1/4 Jigger Lemon Juice

Shake well with ice and strain into glass.

Havana Club

1 Jigger Gold Label Rum
1/2 Jigger Dry Vermouth

Stir well with ice and strain into glass.

Honeybee

1-1/2 Jiggers Light Rum
1/3 Jigger Lemon Juice
1 Tablespoon Honey

Shake well with ice and strain into glass.

Honeysuckle

1 Jigger Gold Label Rum
1 Teaspoon Honey
Juice of 1/2 Lime or Lemon

Shake very well with ice and strain into glass.

Irish Elegance

4/5 Jigger Jamaica Rum
1/5 Brandy
1 Teaspoon Crème de Violette
1/3 Jigger Pineapple Juice
1/2 Teaspoon Sugar
Juice of 1 Lime

Mix in blender with shaved ice and serve immediately.

Jamaica Ginger

2/3 Jamaica Rum
1/3 Grenadine
3 Dashes Maraschino
3 Dashes Curaçao
1 Dash Angostura Bitters

Shake well with ice and strain into glass.

Joburg

1 Jigger Light Rum
1 Jigger Dubonnet
4 Dashes Orange Bitters

Stir well with ice and strain into glass. Serve with twist of Lemon Peel.

Kicker

2/3 Light Rum
1/3 Calvados or Apple Brandy
2 Dashes Sweet Vermouth

Stir well with ice and strain into glass.

Kingston No. 1

1/2 Jamaica Rum
1/4 Kümmel
1/4 Orange Juice
1 Dash Pimento Dram

Shake well with ice and strain into glass.

Kingston No. 2

1 Jigger Jamaica Rum
1/2 Jigger Gin
Juice of 1/2 Lime or Lemon
1 Teaspoon Grenadine

Shake well with ice and strain into glass.

Knickerbocker Special

2/3 Rum
1/3 Curaçao
1 Slice Pineapple, crushed
1 Teaspoon Orange Juice
1 Teaspoon Lemon Juice
1 Teaspoon Raspberry Syrup

Shake well with ice and strain into glass.

La Florida

1-1/3 Jiggers Bacardi Rum
1 Teaspoon Sugar
1 Teaspoon Maraschino
Juice of 1/2 Lemon
Shaved Ice

Shake well and serve frappé, with a small straw.

Little Princess

1/2 Light Rum
1/2 Sweet Vermouth

Stir well with ice and strain into glass.

Maragato (Special)

1/3 Light Rum
1/3 Dry Vermouth
1/3 Sweet Vermouth
1 Dash Kirsch
Juice of 1/2 Lemon
Juice of 1/3 Lime
1/2 Teaspoon Sugar, dissolved in water

Shake well with ice and strain into glass.

Marvel

3/4 Jamaica Rum
1/8 Grenadine
1/8 Sirop de Citron

Shake well with ice and strain into glass.

Mary Pickford

1/2 Light Rum
1/2 Pineapple Juice
1 Teaspoon Grenadine
1 Dash Maraschino

Stir well with ice and strain into glass.

Melba

1/2 Jigger Light Rum
2 Dashes Pernod
1/2 Jigger Swedish Punch
Juice of 1/2 Lime
2 Dashes Grenadine

Shake well with ice and strain into glass.

Miami

1 Jigger Light Rum
1/2 Jigger White Crème de Menthe
2 or 3 Dashes Lemon Juice

Shake well with ice and strain into glass.

Miami Beach

1 Jigger Light Rum
1/3 Jigger Cointreau
1 Dash Lemon or Lime Juice

Shake well with ice and strain into glass.

Million

2/3 Jamaica Rum
1/3 Lime Juice
1/2 Teaspoon Powdered Sugar
1 Dash Angostura Bitters

Shake well with shaved ice and strain into glass. Serve with a Cherry.

Millionaire No. 2

1/3 Jamaica Rum
1/3 Apricot Brandy
1/3 Sloe Gin
1 Dash Grenadine
Juice of 1 Lime

Shake well with ice and strain into glass.

Morning Rose

1/2 Jigger Light Rum
1/2 Jigger Curaçao
1/3 Jigger Grenadine
1/3 Jigger Lemon Juice

Shake well with ice and strain into glass.

Naked Lady

1/2 Light Rum
1/2 Sweet Vermouth
4 Dashes Apricot Brandy
2 Dashes Grenadine
4 Dashes Lemon Juice

Shake well with ice and strain into glass.

National

1-1/3 Jiggers Light Rum
1/3 Jigger Pineapple Juice
1/3 Jigger Apricot Brandy

Shake well with shaved ice and strain into glass. Serve with Pineapple (stick or wedge) and Cherry.

Nevada

1-1/2 Jiggers Light Rum
Juice of 1/2 Grapefruit
Juice of 1 Lime
1 Dash Angostura Bitters
1 Teaspoon Powdered Sugar

Shake well with ice and strain into glass.

Olympia

1 Jigger Dark Rum
2/3 Jigger Cherry Brandy
Juice of 1/2 Lime

Shake well with ice and strain into glass.

Palmetto

1/2 St. Croix Rum
1/2 Sweet Vermouth
2 Dashes Orange Bitters

Stir well with ice and strain into glass. Serve with twist of Lemon Peel.

Panama

1 Jigger Jamaica Rum
1/2 Jigger Crème de Cacao
1/2 Jigger Cream

Shake well with ice and strain into glass.

Paradise

1-1/2 Jiggers Light Rum
1/2 Jigger Apricot Brandy

Shake well with ice and strain into glass.

Parisian Blonde

1/3 Jamaica Rum
1/3 Curaçao
1/3 Cream

Shake well with ice and strain into glass.

Passion (for 4)

1 Jigger Jamaica Rum
4 Jiggers Light Rum
1 Teaspoon Honey
Juice of 2 Limes

Shake well with ice and strain into glasses.

Pauline

1/2 Rum
1/2 Sweetened Lemon Juice
1 Dash Pernod
1 Grating of Nutmeg

Shake well with ice and strain into glass.

Pilgrim

1 Jigger New England Rum
1 Teaspoon Grenadine
Juice of 1/2 Lime or Lemon

Shake well with ice and strain into glass.

Pirate's

2 Parts Dark Rum
1 Sweet Vermouth
1 Dash Angostura Bitters

Stir well with ice and strain into glass.

Planter's No. 1

1/2 Rum
1/2 Orange Juice
1 Dash Lemon Juice

Shake well with ice and strain into glass.

Planter's No. 2

1/2 Dark Rum
1/4 Lemon Juice
1/4 Sugar Syrup

Stir well with ice and strain into glass.

Planter's Punch (see Index)

Platinum Blonde

1 Part Light Rum
1 Cointreau
1/3 Jigger Cream

Shake well with ice and strain into glass.

Poker (see Little Princess)

President

1 Jigger Light Rum
Juice of 1/4 Orange
2 Dashes Grenadine

Shake well with ice and strain into glass.

Quarter Deck No. 1

2/3 Dark Rum
1/3 Sherry
1 Teaspoon Lime Juice

Stir well with ice and strain into glass.

Quarter Deck No. 2

1/2 Jamaica Rum
1/4 Dry Sherry
1/4 Scotch Whisky
1 Teaspoon Sugar Syrup
1 Dash Orange Bitters

Shake well with ice and strain into glass.

Robson

1/2 Jamaica Rum
1/4 Grenadine
1/8 Orange Juice
1/8 Lemon Juice

Shake well with ice and strain into glass.

Royal Bermuda

2 Ounces Barbados Rum
Juice 1 Lime
Little Sugar Syrup
1 Dash Cointreau

Shake with shaved ice and strain into glass.

Rum Dubonnet

1/2 Jigger Light Rum
1/2 Jigger Dubonnet
Juice of 1/2 Lime

Stir well with ice and strain into glass.

Rum Frappé

Place 1 scoop Orange or Lemon Sherbet in a Champagne glass and cover with Rum as desired. Stir and serve.

Rummy

1 Ounce Jamaica Rum
1 Ounce Dry Vermouth
1/2 Ounce Lime Juice
1/2 Ounce Grenadine

Shake well with ice and strain into glass.

Rum Old-Fashioned

Place 1 small lump Sugar in Old-Fashioned glass and sprinkle with a few drops of Angostura or Orange Bitters. Add 1 large twist Lemon Peel and fill glass with ice cubes. Pour in Rum as desired and muddle. A slice of Lemon or Orange or a Cherry may be added.

Rum-on-the-Rocks

Fill Old - Fashioned glass with cracked ice. Pour Rum in as desired. Serve with Lemon Peel.

Rum Sour

2 Jiggers Jamaica Rum
Juice of 1 Lime
Sugar Syrup to taste

Shake well with shaved ice and strain into Delmonico glass. Add slice of Orange and Cherry if desired.

Santiago

2 Jiggers Bacardi Rum
2 Dashes Grenadine
4 Dashes Lime Juice

Stir well with ice and strain into glass.

Saxon

1 Jigger Bacardi Rum
2 Dashes Grenadine
1 Twist Orange Peel
Juice of 1/2 Lime

Shake well with ice and strain into glass.

September Morn

2 Jiggers Bacardi Rum
3 Dashes Grenadine
Juice of 1/2 Lime
1 Egg White

Shake well with ice and strain into glass.

Sevilla No. 1

1/2 Dark Rum
1/2 Sweet Vermouth
1 Twist Orange Peel

Stir well with ice and strain into glass.

Sevilla No. 2

1/2 Light Rum
1/2 Port
1 Egg
1/2 Teaspoon Powdered Sugar

Shake well with ice and strain into glass.

Shanghai

1 Jigger Jamaica Rum
2/3 Ounce Lemon Juice
1/3 Ounce Anisette
2 Dashes Grenadine

Stir well with ice and strain into glass.

Sonora

1/2 Bacardi Rum
1/2 Calvados or Applejack
2 Dashes Apricot Brandy
1 Dash Lemon Juice

Stir well with ice and strain into glass.

Spanish Town

1 Jigger Rum
2 Dashes Curaçao

Shake with shaved ice and strain into glass. Serve with a grating of Nutmeg.

Sunshine No. 2

1/2 Cuban Rum
1/2 Dry Vermouth
2 Dashes Crème de Cassis
Juice of 1 Lime

Stir well with ice and strain into glass.

Sunshine No. 3

Make same as SUNSHINE No. 1, using Bacardi Rum.

Surprised (for 6)

5 Jiggers Jamaica Rum
2-1/2 Jiggers Kümmel
2-1/2 Jiggers Orange Juice
1 Dash Pimento Dram

Shake well with shaved ice and strain into glasses.

Swing

1/3 Bacardi Rum
1/3 Cointreau
1/3 Dry Gin
1 Dash Pernod

Shake well with shaved ice and strain into glass.

Tanglefoot

1/3 Light Rum
1/3 Swedish Punch
1/6 Orange Juice
1/6 Lemon Juice

Shake well with ice and strain into glass.

Trinidad

1-1/2 Jiggers Trinidad Rum

Juice of 1/2 Lime
1 Teaspoon Powdered Sugar
3 Dashes Angostura Bitters

Shake well with ice and strain into glass.

Wedding March

2 Jiggers Light Rum
Juice of 1/2 Lime
2 Egg Whites
2 Dashes Angostura Bitters

Shake well with ice and strain into glass.

Wedding Night

3 Jiggers Martinique Rum
1/2 Jigger Maple Syrup
1 Jigger Lime Juice

Shake with shaved ice and strain into Champagne glass.

West Indies

Add Pineapple Juice to taste to DAIQUIRI (frozen).

White Lion

1 Jigger Dark Rum
Juice of 1/2 Lemon
1 Teaspoon Powdered Sugar
3 Dashes Angostura Bitters
3 Dashes Raspberry Syrup

Shake well with ice and strain into glass.

X.Y.Z.

1/2 Dark Rum
1/4 Cointreau
1/4 Lemon Juice

Shake well with ice and strain into glass.

Yo Ho

1/3 Rum
1/3 Swedish Punch
1/3 Calvados or Apple Brandy

Shake well with ice and strain into glass. Serve with twist of Lemon Peel.

Zombie **(see Long Drinks)**

VODKA BASE

Barbara or Russian Bear

1/2 Vodka
1/4 Crème de Cacao
1/4 Cream

Stir well with ice and strain into glass.

Bloody Mary

1 Jigger Vodka
2 Jiggers Tomato Juice
1/3 Jigger Lemon Juice
1 Dash Worcestershire Sauce
Salt and Pepper to taste

Shake well with ice and strain into glass.

Blue Monday or Caucasian

3/4 Vodka
1/4 Cointreau
1 Dash Blue Vegetable Extract (coloring)

Stir well with ice and strain into glass. Coloring may be omitted.

Golden Screw or Golden Spike

1 Jigger Vodka
3 Jiggers Orange Juice

Shake with ice and strain into glass or serve in tall glass with ice cubes.

Kangaroo

1 Jigger Vodka
1/2 Jigger Dry Vermouth

Stir with cracked ice and strain into glass. Serve with twist of Lemon Peel.

Russian

1 Jigger Vodka
1 Jigger Dry Gin
1 Jigger Crème de Cacao

Stir well with ice and strain into glass.

Tovarich

1 Jigger Vodka
2/3 Jigger Kümmel
Juice of 1/2 Lime

Shake with cracked ice and strain into glass.

Vodka

1 Jigger Vodka
1/2 Jigger Cherry Brandy
Juice of 1/2 Lemon or Lime

Shake with ice and strain into glass.

Vodka Gibson

2 Jiggers Vodka
1/2 Jigger Dry Vermouth

Stir well with ice and strain into glass. Serve with Pickled Pearl Onion.

Vodka Martini

4 or 5 Parts Vodka
1 Part Dry Vermouth

Stir well with ice and strain into glass. Serve with a twist of Lemon Peel.

Vodka-on-the-Rocks

Fill Old-Fashioned glass with ice cubes. Fill with Vodka as desired, and serve with a twist of Lemon Peel.

Volga Boatman

1 Jigger Vodka
1 Jigger Cherry Brandy
1 Jigger Orange Juice

Stir well with ice and strain into glass.

COCKTAILS

WHISKEY BASE

Note: Cocktails with Sugar and/or fruit in an Old-Fashioned glass should always be served with a muddler or a small spoon.

Affinity

1/3 Scotch Whisky
1/3 Dry Vermouth
1/3 Sweet Vermouth
2 Dashes Angostura Bitters

Stir well with ice and strain into glass. Serve with a Cherry and twist a Lemon Peel over top of glass.

Alice

1/3 Scotch Whisky
1/3 Kümmel
1/3 Sweet Vermouth

Stir well with ice and strain into glass.

Appetizer No. 3

2 Jiggers Rye Whiskey
3 Dashes Curaçao
2 Dashes Peychaud's Bitters
1 Twist each Lemon and Orange Peel

Shake well with ice and strain into glass.

Artist's Special

1/3 Whiskey
1/3 Sherry
1/6 Lemon Juice
1/6 Sugar Syrup

Stir well with ice and strain into glass.

Automobile

1/3 Scotch Whisky
1/3 Dry Gin
1/3 Sweet Vermouth
1 Dash Orange Bitters

Stir well with ice and strain into glass.

Barney French

Place 1 slice Orange, 2 dashes Peychaud's Bitters, 1 twist Lemon Peel, 1 or 2 cubes Ice in an Old-Fashioned glass and muddle well. Add 1 or 2 jiggers Whiskey and serve.

Blackthorn

1/2 Irish Whiskey
1/2 Dry Vermouth
3 Dashes Pernod
3 Dashes Angostura Bitters

Stir well with ice and strain into glass.

Blinker

1 Jigger Rye Whiskey
1-1/2 Jiggers Grapefruit Juice
1/2 Jigger Grenadine

Shake well with ice and strain into glass.

Blood and Sand

1/4 Scotch Whisky
1/4 Cherry Brandy
1/4 Sweet Vermouth
1/4 Orange Juice

Stir well with ice and strain into glass.

Blues (for 6)

8 Jiggers Whiskey
2 Jiggers Curaçao
1 Teaspoon Syrup of Prunes

Shake very well with shaved ice and strain into glassses.

Bobby Burns

1/2 Scotch Whisky
1/4 Dry Vermouth
1/4 Sweet Vermouth
1 Dash Benedictine

Stir well with ice and strain into glass.

Boilermaker

Serve 1 large jigger of Whiskey straight, with a Beer chaser on the side.

Boomerang

1/3 Rye Whiskey
1/3 Swedish Punch
1/3 Dry Vermouth
1 Dash Angostura Bitters
1 Dash Lemon Juice

Stir well with ice and strain into glass.

Brainstorm

2 Jiggers Irish Whiskey
2 Dashes Dry Vermouth
2 Dashes Benedictine
1 Twist Orange Peel

Place ingredients in Old-Fashioned glass with ice cubes.

Brooklyn

2/3 Rye Whiskey
1/3 Dry Vermouth
1 Dash Maraschino
1 Dash Amer Picon

Stir well with ice and strain into glass.

Cablegram

2 Jiggers Rye Whiskey
1 Teaspoon Powdered Sugar
Juice of 1/2 Lemon

Stir well with ice and strain into large cocktail glass and fill with dash of Ginger Ale.

Cameron's Kick

1/3 Scotch Whisky
1/3 Irish Whiskey
1/6 Lemon Juice
1/6 Orgeat Syrup

Stir well with ice and strain into glass.

Canadian No. 2

1 Jigger Canadian Club Whiskey
1 Dash Curaçao
2 Dashes Angostura Bitters
1 Teaspoon Powdered Sugar

Shake well with ice and strain into glass.

Capetown

1/2 Rye Whiskey
1/2 Dubonnet
3 Dashes Curaçao
1 Dash Angostura Bitters

Stir well with ice and strain into glass. Serve with twist of Lemon Peel.

Choker (for 6)

8 Jiggers Whiskey
4 Jiggers Pernod
1 Dash Bitters

Shake very well with shaved ice and strain into glasses.

Commodore

2 Jiggers Rye Whiskey
Juice of 1/2 Lime or 1/4 Lemon
2 Dashes Orange Bitters
1 Teaspoon Sugar Syrup

Shake well with ice and strain into glass.

Corn Popper (for 10)

1 Pint Corn Whiskey
1 Cup Cream
2 Egg Whites
1 Tablespoon Grenadine

Shake without ice and fill cocktail glasses 1/2 full. Add 1 ice cube to each and fill with Soda Water.

Cowboy

2/3 Whiskey
1/3 Cream

Shake with shaved ice and strain into glass.

Creole

1/2 Whiskey
1/2 Sweet Vermouth
2 Dashes Benedictine
2 Amer Picon

Stir with ice and strain into glass. Serve with twist of Lemon Peel.

Crow

2/3 Whiskey
1/3 Lemon Juice
1 Dash Grenadine

Stir well with ice and strain into glass.

Dandy

1/2 Rye Whiskey
1/2 Dubonnet
1 Dash Angostura Bitters
3 Dashes Cointreau
1 Twist each Lemon and Orange Peel

Stir well with ice and strain into glass.

Derby No. 2

1/2 Whiskey
1/4 Sweet Vermouth
1/4 White Curaçao
Juice of 1/2 Lime

Shake well with ice and strain into glass. Garnish with a Mint leaf

De Rigueur

1/2 Whiskey
1/4 Grapefruit Juice
1/4 Honey

Shake well with ice and strain into glass.

Deshler

1 Jigger Rye Whiskey
1 Jigger Dubonnet
2 Dashes Peychaud's Bitters
2 Dashes Cointreau
2 Twists Orange Peel
1 Twist Lemon Peel

Shake well with ice and strain into glass. Serve with a twist of Orange Peel.

Dinah (for 6)

6 Jiggers Whiskey
6 Jiggers Sweetened Lemon Juice
3 Sprigs Fresh Mint, slightly bruised

Shake with shaved ice and strain into glasses. Garnish with Mint leaves.

Dixie (for 6)

6 Jiggers Rye Whiskey
2 Teaspoons Sugar
2 Dashes Angostura Bitters
1 Teaspoon Lemon Juice
1 Teaspoon Curaçao
2 Teaspoons White Crème de Menthe

Shake well with ice and strain into glasses. Garnish with Mint leaves.

Duppy (for 6)

Pour 6 jiggers of Whiskey into a mixing glass and add a few Cloves. Let soak for about 1 hour. Add 5 or 6 drops Orange Bitters and 1 jigger Curaçao. Shake well with ice and strain into glasses.

Earthquake

1/3 Whiskey
1/3 Gin
1/3 Pernod

Shake well with ice and strain into glass.

Edward VIII

Place in an Old-Fashioned glass 2 jiggers Rye Whiskey, 1 dash Pernod and 2 teaspoons each Sweet Vermouth and Water. Add 1 or 2 ice cubes and twist of Orange Peel. Stir and serve.

Elk's Own

1/2 Rye Whiskey
1/2 Port
1 Egg White
Juice of 1/2 Lemon
1 Teaspoon Sugar

Shake well with ice and

strain into glass. Serve with small wedge of Pineapple.

Evans

2 Jiggers Rye Whiskey
1 Dash Apricot Brandy
1 Dash Curaçao

Stir with ice and strain.

Evening Gun (see Duppy)

Everybody's Irish

1 Jigger Irish Whiskey
6 Dashes Green Chartreuse
3 Dashes Green Crème de Menthe

Stir well with ice and strain into glass. Serve with Green Olive.

Everything But

1/4 Whiskey
1/4 Gin
1/4 Lemon Juice
1/4 Orange Juice
1 Egg
1 Teaspoon Apricot Brandy
1/2 Teaspoon Powdered Sugar

Shake well with ice and strain into glass.

Fans

2/3 Jigger Scotch Whisky
1/3 Jigger Cointreau
1/3 Jigger Unsweetened Grapefruit Juice

Shake well with ice and strain into glass.

Flu

2 Jiggers Rye Whiskey
1 Teaspoon Ginger Brandy
1 Teaspoon Rock Candy Syrup
1 Pinch Jamaica Rum
Juice of 1/4 Lemon

Stir well without ice and strain into glass. This is supposedly a medicine.

Flying Scot (for 6)

6 Jiggers Scotch Whisky
4 Jiggers Sweet Vermouth
1 Tablespoon Sugar Syrup
1 Tablespoon Bitters

Shake well with ice and strain into glasses.

Fox River

3/4 Rye Whiskey
1/4 Crème de Cacao
4 Dashes Peach Bitters

Stir gently with a little ice and strain into glass. Squeeze Lemon Peel over top.

Frisco

1 Jigger Bourbon Whiskey
1/2 Jigger Benedictine

Stir with shaved ice and strain into glass. Serve with twist of Lemon Peel.

Grace's Delight (for 6)

4 Jiggers Whiskey
5 Jiggers Dry Vermouth
1 Jigger Framboise
Juice of 1/2 Orange
1 Teaspoon Orange Bitters
1 Teaspoon Orange Flower Water
1 Pinch Cinnamon
1 Pinch Nutmeg
3 Juniper Berries

Combine all ingredients in shaker and place on ice for 1 hour. Shake without ice and strain into glasses.

Harry Lauder

1/2 Scotch Whisky
1/2 Sweet Vermouth
2 Dashes Sugar Syrup

Stir well with ice and strain into glass.

Highland Fling

1 Jigger Scotch Whisky
1 Teaspoon Sugar
2 Jiggers Milk

Shake very well with ice and strain into Delmonico glass. Sprinkle Nutmeg on top.

"Hoots Mon"

1/2 Scotch Whisky
1/4 Lillet
1/4 Sweet Vermouth

Stir well with ice and strain into glass.

Hot Deck

3/4 Rye Whiskey
1/4 Sweet Vermouth
1 Dash Jamaica Ginger

Shake well with ice and strain into glass.

Hurricane

1/2 Jigger Rye or Bourbon Whiskey
1/2 Jigger White Crème de Menthe
1/2 Jigger Dry Gin
Juice of 1 Lemon

Shake well with ice and strain into glass.

Ink Street

1/2 Rye Whiskey
1/4 Orange Juice
1/4 Lemon Juice

Shake well with ice and strain into glass.

Irish

1 Jigger Irish Whiskey
2 Dashes Pernod
2 Dashes Curaçao
1 Dash Maraschino
1 Dash Angostura Bitters

Stir well with ice and strain. Squeeze Orange Peel on top.

John Wood (see Serpent's Tooth)

King Cole

1 Jigger Bourbon Whiskey
1 Dash Fernet Branca
2 Dashes Sugar Syrup
1 Slice Orange
1 Slice Pineapple
1 Lump Ice

Muddle all ingredients well.

Kitchen Sink

1/4 Rye Whiskey
1/4 Gin
1/4 Lemon Juice
1/4 Orange Juice
1 Egg
1 Teaspoon Apricot Brandy
1/2 Teaspoon Powdered Sugar

Shake well with ice and strain into glass.

Ladies'

1 Jigger Whiskey
2 Dashes Pernod
3 Dashes Anisette
1 Dash Angostura Bitters

Stir well with ice and strain into glass. Serve with a piece of Pineapple on top.

Lawhill

2/3 Rye Whiskey
1/3 Dry Vermouth
1 Dash Pernod
1 Dash Maraschino
1 Dash Angostura Bitters

Stir well with ice and strain into glass.

Linstead (for 6)

6 Jiggers Whiskey
6 Jiggers Sweetened Pineapple Juice
1 Dash Bitters

Shake well in ice and strain into glasses. Squeeze Lemon Peel over top.

Loch Lomond

1 Jigger Scotch Whisky
3 Dashes Angostura Bitters
1 Teaspoon Sugar

Shake well with ice and strain into glass.

London

1 Jigger Rye Whiskey
1/4 Jigger Orgeat Syrup
2 Dashes Orange Flower Water
1 Egg

Shake well with ice and strain into glass. Serve with sprinkling of Nutmeg.

Los Angeles (for 4)

4 Large Jiggers Whiskey
Juice of 1 Lemon
4 Teaspoons Sugar
1 Egg
1 Dash Sweet Vermouth

Shake well with ice and strain into glasses.

Manhattan (Dry)

4 Parts Whiskey
1 Part Dry Vermouth
1 Dash Bitters

Stir very well with ice and strain into glass. Add a twist of Lemon Peel or a Cherry.

Manhattan (Sweet)

2/3 Whiskey
1/6 Sweet Vermouth
1/6 Dry Vermouth
1 Dash Bitters

Stir well with ice and strain into glass. Serve with a Cherry (optional).

Master of the Hounds

1 Jigger Rye Whiskey
1/3 Jigger Cherry Brandy
2 Dashes Angostura Bitters

Stir well with ice and strain into glass.

Mickie Walker

3 Parts Scotch Whisky

1 Part Sweet Vermouth
1 Dash Lemon Juice
1 Dash Grenadine

Shake well with ice and strain into glass.

Millionaire No. 3

1 Jigger Bourbon
1/3 Jigger Curaçao
1 Egg White
1 Dash Grenadine

Shake well with shaved ice and strain into large cocktail glass.

Modern No. 2

2 Jiggers Scotch Whisky
1 Dash Lemon Juice
1 Dash Pernod
2 Dashes Jamaica Rum
1 Dash Orange Bitters

Stir well with ice, strain into glass and serve with a Cherry.

Monte Carlo

1 Jigger Rye Whiskey
1/3 Jigger Benedictine
2 Dashes Angostura Bitters

Shake well with ice and strain into glass.

Morning Glory

2/3 Jigger Whiskey
2/3 Jigger Brandy
1 Dash Pernod
2 Dashes Bitters
2 Dashes Curaçao
3 Dashes Sugar Syrup
1 Twist Lemon Peel

Place ingredients in large cocktail glass, with 1–2 pieces of ice. Stir and remove ice. Fill glass with Soda Water and stir with a teaspoon coated with Powdered Sugar.

Mountain

1/2 Rye Whiskey
1/6 Lemon Juice
1/6 Dry Vermouth
1/6 Sweet Vermouth
1 Egg White

Shake well with ice and strain into glass.

Mud Pie

In an Old-Fashioned glass muddle 1/2 cube Sugar with 2 dashes Peychaud's Bitters, 4 dashes Curaçao and 1 large cube ice. Decorate with fruit, if desired, and serve with 1 jigger Whiskey on the side.

New Orleans

1 Jigger Bourbon
1 Dash Orange Bitters
2 Dashes Angostura Bitters
1 Dash Anisette
2 Dashes Pernod
1/2 Lump Sugar

Stir well with ice and strain into glass. Serve with twist of Lemon Peel.

New York

1-1/2 Jiggers Rye Whiskey
1/2 Teaspoon Powdered Sugar
1 Dash Grenadine
Juice of 1/2 Lime
1 Twist Orange Peel

Shake well with ice and strain into glass.

Oh, Henry!

1/3 Whiskey
1/3 Benedictine
1/3 Ginger Ale

Stir well with ice and strain into glass.

Old-Fashioned

Place in an Old-Fashioned glass 1 lump of Sugar. Sprinkle it with a light dash of Angostura Bitters. Add ice cubes and twist of Lemon Peel (Maraschino Cherry and Orange Slice, if desired) and fill with Whiskey, any Whiskey.

Old Pal

1/3 Rye Whiskey
1/3 Dry Vermouth
1/3 Campari

Stir well with ice and strain into glass.

Old Pepper

1-1/3 Jiggers Whiskey
Juice of 1/2 Lemon
1 Teaspoon Worcestershire Sauce
1 Teaspoon Chili Sauce
2 Dashes Angostura Bitters
1 Dash Tabasco Sauce

Shake well with ice and serve in Delmonico glass.

Old Time Appetizer

1/2 Jigger Rye or Bourbon
1/2 Jigger Dubonnet
2 Dashes Curaçao
2 Dashes Pernod
1 Slice Orange
1 Slice Pineapple
1 Twist Lemon Peel
1 Dash Peychaud's Bitters

Place all together in Old-Fashioned glass with ice cubes, and serve with a muddler.

Opening

1/2 Rye Whiskey
1/4 Sweet Vermouth
1/4 Grenadine

Stir well with ice and strain into glass.

Oppenheim

1/2 Jigger Bourbon
1/4 Jigger Grenadine
1/4 Jigger Sweet Vermouth

Stir well with ice and strain into glass.

Oriental (see Derby)

Paddy

1/2 Irish Whiskey
1/2 Sweet Vermouth
1 Dash Angostura Bitters

Stir well with ice and strain into glass.

Palmer

1 Jigger Rye Whiskey
1 Dash Angostura Bitters
1 Dash Lemon Juice

Stir well with ice and strain into glass.

Pick-Up

2/3 Rye Whiskey
1/3 Fernet Branca
3 Dashes Pernod
1 Slice Lemon

Stir gently with a little ice and strain into glass.

Polly's Special

1/2 Scotch Whisky
1/4 Unsweetened Grapefruit Juice
1/4 Curaçao

Shake well with ice and strain into glass.

Quaker

1/2 Rye Whiskey
1/2 Brandy
1 Teaspoon Raspberry Syrup
Juice of 1/2 Lime

Shake well with ice and strain into glass.

Rah-Rah-Rut

1 Jigger Rye Whiskey
2 Dashes Pernod
2 Dashes Peychaud's Bitters

Stir well with ice and strain into glass.

Rattlesnake (for 6)

8 Jiggers Rye Whiskey
2 Egg Whites
2 Jiggers Sweetened Lemon Juice
3 Dashes Pernod

Shake well with ice and strain into glass.

Rob Roy

1 Jigger Scotch Whisky
2/3 Jigger Sweet Vermouth
2 Dashes Angostura Bitters

Stir well with ice and strain into glass. Serve with twist of Lemon Peel.

Rock and Rye

Dissolve 1 piece of Rock Candy in 2 jiggers of Rye Whiskey. Lemon Juice may be added if desired.

Russell House (Down the Hatch)

2 Jiggers Rye Whiskey
3 Dashes Blackberry Brandy
2 Dashes Sugar Syrup
2 Dashes Orange Bitters

Stir well with ice and strain into glass.

Rye Whiskey

2 Jiggers Rye Whiskey
4 Dashes Sugar Syrup
1 Dash Angostura Bitters

Stir well with ice and strain into glass. Serve with a Cherry.

Sazerac

1 Jigger Rye Whiskey
1 Dash Pernod
1 Dash Peychaud's Bitters
1 Lump Sugar, dissolved in 1 teaspoon Water

Stir well with ice and strain into a chilled glass. Squeeze Lemon Peel over top.

Scoff-Law

1/3 Rye Whiskey
1/3 Dry Vermouth
1/6 Lemon Juice
1/6 Grenadine
1 Dash Orange Bitters

Stir well with ice and strain into glass.

Scotch Mist

Fill Old-Fashioned glass with shaved ice. Pour in Scotch Whisky as desired. Add twist of Lemon Peel.

Note: Any other Whiskey may be used.

Scotch-on-the-Rocks

Fill Old-Fashioned glass with ice cubes. Pour in Whiskey as desired, with or without water, and with or without twist of Lemon Peel.

Scotch Side Car

1 Jigger Scotch Whisky
1/2 Jigger Cointreau
1/2 Jigger Lemon Juice

Shake well with ice and strain into large cocktail glass.

Note: Any Whiskey, Straight or Blended, may be substituted.

Serpent's Tooth (John Wood)

2 Parts Irish Whiskey
4 Parts Sweet Vermouth
2 Parts Lemon Juice
1 Part Kümmel
1 Dash Angostura Bitters

Stir well with ice and strain into glass.

"S. G."

1/3 Rye Whiskey
1/3 Lemon Juice
1/3 Orange Juice
1 Teaspoon Grenadine

Shake well with ice and strain into glass.

Shamrock—Friendly Sons of St. Patrick

1/2 Irish Whiskey
1/2 Dry Vermouth
3 Dashes Green Chartreuse
3 Dashes Green Crème de Menthe

Stir well with ice and strain into glass. Serve with Green Olive.

Soul Kiss No. 2

1/3 Rye Whiskey
1/3 Dry Vermouth
1/6 Dubonnet
1/6 Orange Juice
1 Slice Orange

Stir well with ice and strain into glass.

Southside

Muddle in a mixing glass or shaker a few fresh Mint leaves with 1 teaspoon Powdered Sugar. Add Juice of 1/2 Lemon and 1-1/2 jiggers Bourbon. Shake thoroughly with ice and strain into glass.

Note: This may also be made with Gin.

S. S. Manhattan

1/2 Bourbon Whiskey
1/2 Orange Juice
1 Dash Benedictine

Shake well with ice and strain into glass.

Temptation

1 Jigger Rye Whiskey
2 Dashes Curaçao
2 Dashes Pernod
2 Dashes Dubonnet
1 Twist each Orange and Lemon Peel

Stir well with ice and strain into glass.

Thistle

1/2 Scotch Whisky
1/2 Sweet Vermouth
2 Dashes Angostura Bitters

Stir well with ice and strain into glass.

Tipperary No. 2

1/3 Irish Whiskey
1/3 Chartreuse
1/3 Sweet Vermouth

Stir well with ice and strain into glass.

T.N.T.

1/2 Rye Whiskey
1/2 Pernod

Shake well with ice and strain into glass.

Tom Moore

2/3 Irish Whiskey
1/3 Sweet Vermouth
1 Dash Angostura Bitters

Stir well with ice and strain into glass.

Trilby No. 2

1/3 Scotch Whisky
1/3 Sweet Vermouth
1/3 Parfait Amour Liqueur
2 Dashes Orange Bitters
2 Dashes Pernod

Stir well with ice and strain into glass.

Up-to-Date

1/2 Rye Whiskey
1/2 Sherry
2 Dashes Angostura Bitters
2 Dashes Grand Marnier

Stir well with ice and strain into glass.

Waldorf No. 2

1/3 Bourbon Whiskey
1/3 Pernod
1/3 Sweet Vermouth
3 Dashes Angostura Bitters

Stir well with ice and strain into glass.

Ward Eight No. 2

1 Jigger Rye or Bourbon Whiskey
2 or 4 Dashes Grenadine

Shake well with ice and strain into goblet. Add extra ice and fruit garnish as desired. Serve with straws.

Wembley No. 2

1/3 Scotch Whisky
1/3 Dry Vermouth
1/3 Pineapple Juice

Shake well with ice and strain into glass.

Whiskey

1 or 2 Jiggers Rye or Bourbon Whiskey
1 or 3 Dashes Angostura Bitters
1 Dash Sugar Syrup

Stir well with ice and strain into large cocktail glass.

Whiskey and Bitters

Same as WHISKEY, omitting Sugar Syrup. Generally served with ice in glass.

Whiskey and Honey

Place in Old-Fashioned glass 1 teaspoon Honey, 1 or 2 ice cubes, 1 twist Lemon Peel. Pour in 1 or 2 jiggers

Whiskey. Serve with muddler and drink immediately.

Whiskey on Rocks

Place ice cubes in Old-Fashioned glass and pour in any Whiskey desired, with or without water.

Whiskey Sour

1 or 2 Jiggers any Whiskey
Juice of 1/2 Lemon
1/2 Teaspoon Sugar

Shake well with ice and serve in Delmonico glass, garnished with Cherry and Orange slice if desired. The proportion of Whiskey and Sugar may be altered to suit individual taste.

Whiskey Special (for 6)

6 Jiggers Whiskey
4 Jiggers Dry Vermouth
1 Jigger Orange Juice
1 Pinch Nutmeg

Shake well with ice and strain into glasses. Serve with a twist of Orange Peel.

Whisper

1/3 Whiskey
1/3 Dry Vermouth
1/3 Sweet Vermouth

Shake well with ice and strain into glass.

White Shadow

1/3 Rye Whiskey
1/3 Pernod
1/3 Cream
1 Pinch Nutmeg

Shake well with shaved ice and strain into glass.

Whizz Bang

2/3 Scotch Whisky
1/3 Dry Vermouth
2 Dashes Orange Bitters
2 Dashes Grenadine
2 Dashes Pernod

Stir well with ice and strain into glass.

Wild-Eyed Rose

2 Jiggers Irish Whiskey
1/2 Jigger Grenadine
Juice of 1/2 Lime

Place ingredients in large cocktail glass with 1 ice cube and fill with Soda Water.

Yashmak

1/3 Rye Whiskey
1/3 Pernod
1/3 Dry Vermouth
1 Dash Angostura Bitters
1 or 2 Pinches Sugar

Stir well with ice and strain into glass.

Zazarac

1/3 Rye Whiskey
1/6 Sugar Syrup
1/6 Anisette
1/6 Light Rum
1/6 Pernod
1 Dash Orange Bitters
1 Dash Angostura Bitters

Shake well with ice and strain into glass. Squeeze Lemon Peel on top.

COLLINS

TOM AND JOHN

The Collins is generally made in a highball glass. Its basic proportions are 2 or 3 cubes of ice, the juice of 1/2 or 1 Lemon, 1 or 1-1/2 teaspoons Sugar and 1 or 2 jiggers of any of the following liquors: Applejack, Brandy, Gin, Rum, Whiskey or Vodka.

The proportions are a matter of personal taste, depending on the strength and sweetness of drink desired.

The TOM COLLINS is a GIN COLLINS. The JOHN COLLINS uses Holland Gin.

Applejack Cooler

1 Tablespoon Sugar
Juice of 1/2 Lemon
1 or 2 Jiggers Applejack

Shake well with cracked ice and strain into highball glass. Add ice cubes and fill with chilled Soda Water.

Apricot Cooler

1 Jigger Apricot Brandy
Juice of 1/2 each Lemon and Lime
2 Dashes Grenadine

Shake well with cracked ice and strain into highball glass and fill with Soda Water.

Bishop's Cooler

Place in large highball glass 2 jiggers Burgundy, 1/2 jigger Dark Rum, 1/3 jigger Orange Juice, 1/3 Lemon Juice, 1 teaspoon Sugar, 2 dashes Angostura Bitters. Fill with shaved ice, stir and serve.

Country Club Cooler

2 Jiggers Dry Vermouth
1 Teaspoon Grenadine

Place in tall glass with ice and fill with chilled Soda Water.

Cuban Cooler

Place ice cubes in a tall highball glass and add 1 or 2 jiggers Rum and fill with Ginger Ale. Garnish with twist of Lemon Peel.

Harvard Cooler

Place in a shaker with ice 1 tablespoon Sugar Syrup, juice of 1/2 Lemon and 1 or 2 jiggers Applejack. Shake well and strain into tall highball glass. Fill with chilled Soda Water.

Hawaiian Cooler

Place ice cubes in a large tumbler or highball glass and add a long twist of Orange Peel, 1 or 2 jiggers Rye Whiskey and fill with chilled Soda Water.

Highland Cooler

Place ice cubes in a tall glass and add 2 jiggers Scotch Whisky, 2 dashes Angostura Bitters, juice of 1/2 Lemon and 1 teaspoon Powdered Sugar. Stir and fill with chilled Ginger Ale.

Irish Cooler

Place ice cubes in a large tumbler or highball glass with a long twist of Lemon Peel. Add 1 or 2 jiggers Irish Whiskey and fill with Soda Water.

Lone Tree

The same as APRICOT COOLER, but with a little more Lemon Juice and a little less Grenadine.

Long Tom Cooler

The same as TOM COLLINS, but always with 1 slice of Orange.

Manhattan Cooler

Place in a tall glass 2 or 3 jiggers Claret, 3 dashes Rum, juice of 1/2 Lemon and 1 or 2 teaspoons Powdered Sugar. Add ice and decorate with fruit if desired.

Mint Cooler

Place ice in highball glass and add 2 jiggers Scotch Whisky, 3 dashes White Crème de Menthe and fill with Soda Water.

Moonlight

2 or 3 Jiggers Calvados or Applejack
Juice of 1 Lemon
1-1/2 Teaspoons Sugar

Shake well with shaved ice and strain into tall glass. Fill with chilled Soda Water. Decorate with fruit if desired.

Orange Blossom Cooler

Shake well with shaved ice 1 or 2 jiggers Dry Gin, juice of 1/2 Orange, 1 teaspoon

Sugar and strain into highball glass, filling with iced Soda Water. Garnish with fruit or Mint.

Red Wine Cooler

Dissolve 2 teaspoons Sugar in a very little water. Add 4 teaspoons Orange Juice and place in highball glass with ice cubes. Fill with any Red Wine and garnish with Lemon Slice.

Remsen Cooler

2 Jiggers Scotch Whisky
   or Dry Gin
1 Lemon
Soda Water

Peel off the rind of the Lemon in as long a twist as possible and place in highball glass with ice. Add liquor as desired and fill with Soda Water.

Scotch Cooler

Place in a highball glass 1 or 2 jiggers Scotch Whisky, 3 dashes Crème de Menthe and ice cubes. Fill with chilled Soda Water.

Scotch Stone Fence

Place 2 jiggers Scotch Whisky and 2 dashes Peychaud's Bitters in a highball glass with 1 small twist of Lemon Peel and ice cubes. Fill with Soda Water.

Sea Breeze

Place in a highball glass 1 jigger Dry Gin, 1 jigger Apricot Brandy, 1 dash Grenadine, juice of 1/2 Lemon and ice cubes. Fill with chilled Soda Water and decorate with sprigs of Mint.

Shady Grove

In a highball glass combine 2 jiggers Dry Gin, juice of 1/2 Lemon and 1-1/2 teaspoons Sugar. Add ice cubes and fill with Ginger Beer.

Whiskey Cooler

Place in a highball glass 2 jiggers Rye or Bourbon, the juice of 1/2 Lemon, 1 teaspoon Sugar and ice cubes. Fill with chilled Ginger Ale.

White Wine Cooler

Place 1 tablespoon Sugar Syrup and 2 or 3 jiggers chilled Soda Water in a highball glass with ice cubes. Fill with chilled White Wine. Garnish with Mint and, if desired, an Orange slice.

Zenith

Place in a large tumbler several ice cubes with 1 tablespoon Pineapple Juice, 1 or 2 jiggers Dry Gin and fill with Soda Water. Serve with a Pineapple stick.

CRUSTAS

Basic

Crustas may be made of Applejack, Brandy, Gin, Rum or Whiskey. Rub the rim of a large Wineglass with Lemon, then dip glass in Powdered Sugar. Place in the glass a large twist of Lemon or Orange Peel and a Cherry. In a shaker with ice put 1 dash Angostura Bitters, 1 teaspoon each Lemon Juice and Maraschino and 1 or 2 jiggers of the desired liquor. Strain into prepared glass and serve.

Burgundy Cup

2 Jiggers Whiskey
1 Jigger Curaçao
1 Jigger Benedictine
1-1/2 Bottles Burgundy (Red)
1 Pint Soda Water
4 Tablespoons Sugar

Place in large pitcher with ice cubes and stir. Decorate with slices of Orange and Pineapple, Maraschino Cherries, Cucumber rind, and fresh Mint.

Chablis Cup

Place ice cubes in a large pitcher and add: 1 jigger Benedictine, 1 or 2 slices Lemon, 3 thin slices Pineapple, and 1 bottle Chablis (Pouilly or any White Burgundy may be used). Stir gently and serve. Peeled ripe Peaches may be used in place of Pineapple slices.

Cider Cup No. 1

1 Quart Cider
1 Jigger Maraschino
1 Jigger Curaçao
1 Jigger Brandy
Ice Cubes
Soda Water

Fill pitcher with ice cubes and decorate with Lemon or Orange Peel. Add other ingredients and Soda Water as desired.

Cider Cup No. 2 (for 4)

1 Quart Cider
1 Jigger Calvados or Apple Brandy
1 Jigger Brandy
1 Jigger Curaçao
1 Pint Soda Water

Place all together in pitcher with ice cubes and 2 large sprigs Mint. Stir and serve.

Claret Cup (for 10)

1 Bottle Claret (Bordeaux)
1/2 Jigger Maraschino
1/2 Jigger Curaçao
1 Jigger Sugar Syrup

Decorate with Orange and Pineapple, and Mint if desired.

Claret Cup No. 2

Fill a large pitcher 1/2 full of cracked ice. Add 1 jigger Curaçao, 1 jigger Brandy, 1 jigger Sugar Syrup, 1 dash Maraschino, 1 Lemon, sliced thin, 1 Orange, sliced thin, 2 or 3 slices fresh Pineapple, 1/2 pint Soda Water, and 1 or 2 quarts Claret. Stir well. (It is advisable to add the Soda Water just before serving.) Makes 10 to 12 cups.

Empire Peach Cup

Carefully peel 1 or 2 ripe Peaches and slice into a large bowl or pitcher, losing as little juice as possible. Add 1 bottle Moselle and 2 or 3 tablespoons Sugar. Stir and set aside, covered, for 1/2 hour. Add 1 more bottle Moselle and just before serving add ice and 1 bottle Sparkling Moselle. This Cup is perhaps better if no ice is added, but the pitcher or bowl should be set in a bed of crushed ice. Makes 15 to 20 cups.

Grapefruit Cup

Place a large piece of ice in a big pitcher or bowl and add 1 bottle Brandy, 2 jiggers Grenadine, meat of 3 seeded Grapefruits and 1 can of Grapefruit Juice. Stir and decorate with Mint leaves. Just before serving, add 1 small bottle Soda Water. 10 to 12 cups.

Kalte Ente

Place in a large pitcher the whole curled rind of 1 Lemon, 2 jiggers Curaçao, 1 bottle Moselle, chilled, and 1 bottle Sparkling Moselle. 10 to 12 cups.

May Wine

In a large pitcher soak a bunch of Woodruff in 3 bottles Moselle for 1 hour, with a piece of ice. Add 6 lumps

Sugar, 2 jiggers Curaçao, 2 jiggers Brandy and 1 bottle Sparkling Moselle before serving. 25 to 30 cups.

Moselle Cup

Place in a large pitcher a good piece of ice, 3 peeled ripe Peaches, quartered, 12 Maraschino Cherries, 1 jigger Benedictine, 1 bottle Moselle and, just before serving, 1 ice-cold bottle Sparkling Moselle. 10 to 12 cups.

Pfirsich Bowle

Place a large chunk of ice in a big pitcher, with 2 whole ripe Peaches which have been pierced with a fork. Add 1 or 2 bottles light Rhine Wine and Powdered Sugar, if desired. Mint may also be added. 10 to 12 cups.

Rhine Wine Cup

Place a large piece of ice in a big pitcher or punch bowl with slices of Orange, Pineapple, Cucumber Peel and a few Maraschino Cherries. Add 1 jigger Maraschino, 1 jigger Curaçao, 2 bottles Rhine Wine. 10 to 12 cups.

Sauterne Cup

Place a large pitcher or punch bowl in a bed of crushed ice. Combine the ingredients in the order listed:

1 Jigger Brandy
1 Jigger Curaçao
1 Jigger Maraschino
2 Bottles Sauterne, chilled
1/2 Pint chilled Soda Water

Garnish with Lemon and Orange slices. Serves 10 to 12.

Velvet Cup

Prepare same as CHAMPAGNE VELVET, but in a pitcher with ice, pouring in Stout and Champagne carefully so as not to overflow.

DAISIES

Note: Daisies are overgrown Cocktails. They should be served in very large cocktail glasses or goblets. Place the juice of 1/2 Lemon, 1 teaspoon Grenadine and 1 or 2 jiggers of Applejack, Brandy, Gin, Rum or Whiskey in a shaker with shaved ice. Shake well and strain into glass. Fill with chilled Soda Water. Sometimes the White of 1 Egg and a dash of Pernod are added.

Santa Cruz Rum Daisy

Fill a goblet 1/3 full of shaved ice and add 3 dashes Sugar Syrup, 3 dashes Maraschino or Curaçao, juice of 1/2 Lemon and fill with Rum.

FIXES

All Fixes should be served in small tumblers with shaved ice.

Brandy Fix

1 Jigger Brandy
1 Jigger Cherry Brandy
1 Teaspoon Sugar
1 Teaspoon Water
Juice of 1/2 Lemon

Moisten the Sugar with the Water and add the other ingredients. Fill with ice and stir gently. Add a slice of Lemon or twist of Peel. Serve with a straw.

Gin Fix

2 Jiggers Dry Gin
1 Teaspoon Sugar
1 Teaspoon Water
Juice of 1/2 Lemon

Moisten the Sugar with the Water and add other ingredients. Fill with ice and stir gently. Add a slice of Lemon or twist of Peel. Serve with a straw.

Note: The RUM FIX and the WHISKEY FIX are made as above, substituting the desired liquor.

Santa Cruz Fix

The SANTA CRUZ FIX is mado the same as the BRANDY FIX, substituting Rum for the Brandy.

FIZZES

Most Fizzes are served in a 7-ounce highball glass.

Alabama Fizz

Prepare the same as GIN FIZZ, adding a sprig of Mint.

Albemarle

2 Jiggers Dry Gin
1/2 Tablespoon Powdered Sugar
1 Dash Raspberry Syrup
Juice of 1/2 Lemon

Shake well with ice and strain into glass. Fill with Soda Water

American Fizz

1 Jigger Gin
1 Jigger Brandy
Juice of 1/2 Lemon
1 Teaspoon Grenadine

Shake well with ice and strain into glass.

Apple Blow

2 Jiggers Applejack
4 Dashes Lemon Juice
1 Teaspoon Sugar
1 Egg White

Shake well with ice and strain into glass. Fill with Soda Water.

Bacardi Fizz

2 Jiggers Bacardi Rum
1 Teaspoon Sugar
Juice of 1/2 Lemon

Shake well with ice and strain into glass. Fill with Soda Water.

Bismarck Fizz (Sloe Gin Fizz)

2 Jiggers Sloe Gin
Juice of 1/2 Lemon

Shake well with ice and strain into glass. Fill with Soda Water.

Boot Leg

Make same as GIN FIZZ, adding white of 1 Egg and sprigs of Mint.

Brandy Fizz

Make same as GIN FIZZ, using Brandy.

Bucks Fizz

1 Jigger Gin
1/2 Teaspoon Sugar
Juice of 1/2 Orange

Shake well with ice and strain into glass. Fill with chilled Champagne.

Cider Fizz (for 2)

2 Jiggers Gold Label Rum
1/4 Cup Apple Cider
1 Tablespoon Lemon Juice
1 Teaspoon Sugar
1/2 Cup Shaved Ice

Pre - chill the ingredients and place them in the glass container of an electric blender. Cover and turn on for 20 seconds. Place two ice cubes in large highball glasses. Pour in blended mixture and fill with Soda Water or Ginger Ale.

Cream Fizz

Make same as GIN FIZZ with 1 or 2 teaspoons Cream added.

Derby Fizz

1 Jigger Whiskey
5 Dashes Lemon Juice
1 Teaspoon Sugar
1 Egg
3 Dashes Curaçao

Shake well with ice and strain into glass. Fill up with Soda Water.

Diamond Fizz

1 Jigger Gin
1/2 Teaspoon Sugar
Juice of 1/2 Lemon

Shake well with ice and strain into glass. Fill up with Soda Water.

Dubonnet Fizz

2 Jiggers Dubonnet
1 Teaspoon Cherry Brandy
Juice of 1/2 Orange
Juice of 1/4 Lemon

Shake well with ice and strain into glass. Fill up with Soda Water.

Frank's Special Fizz

2 Jiggers Gin
1/4 Crushed Peach
1/2 Teaspoon Sugar
Juice of 1/2 Lemon

Shake well with ice and strain into glass. Fill with Soda Water or chilled Champagne.

Gin Fizz

2 Jiggers Dry Gin
1 Tablespoon Powdered Sugar
Juice of 1/2 Lemon
Juice of 1/2 Lime

Shake well with ice and strain into glass. Fill up with Soda Water.

Golden Fizz

Make same as GIN FIZZ, adding Yolk of 1 Egg.

Grand Royal Fizz

Make same as GIN FIZZ, adding 1 dash Maraschino, 3 dashes Orange Juice and 1/2 jigger Cream.

Grenadine Fizz

2 Jiggers Gin
2 Teaspoons Grenadine
Juice of 1/2 Lemon

Shake well with ice and strain into glass. Fill up with Soda Water.

Hoffman House Fizz

2 Jiggers Dry Gin
Juice of 1/2 Lemon
1 Teaspoon Sugar
1 Teaspoon Cream
2 Dashes Maraschino

Shake well with ice and strain into glass. Fill up with Soda Water.

Holland Gin Fizz

Make same as GIN FIZZ, using Holland Gin.

Imperial Fizz

1 Jigger Rye or Bourbon Whiskey
Juice of 1/2 Lemon
1/2 Teaspoon Sugar

Shake well with ice and strain into glass. Fill with chilled Champagne.

Imperial Hotel Fizz

2/3 Whiskey
1/3 Light Rum
4 Dashes Lemon Juice
Juice of 1/2 Lime

Shake well with ice and strain into glass. Fill with Soda Water.

Irish Fizz

2 Jiggers Irish Whiskey
1 Teaspoon Curaçao
1/2 Teaspoon Sugar
Juice of 1/2 Lemon

Shake well with ice and strain into glass. Fill up with Soda Water.

Jubilee Fizz

1/2 Dry Gin
1/2 Unsweetened Pineapple Juice

Shake well with ice and strain into glass. Fill with chilled Champagne.

May Blossom Fizz

1 Jigger Swedish Punch
1 Teaspoon Grenadine
Juice of 1/2 Lemon

Shake well with ice and strain into glass. Fill up with Soda Water.

Morning Glory Fizz

2 Jiggers Scotch Whisky
2 Dashes Pernod
1 Egg White
1 Teaspoon Powdered Sugar
Juice of 1/2 Lemon
Juice of 1/2 Lime

Shake well with ice and strain into glass. Fill up with Soda Water.

New Orleans Fizz

2 Jiggers Dry Gin
1 Egg White
Juice of 1/2 Lemon
1 Teaspoon Sugar
1 Teaspoon Cream
1 Dash Orange Flower Water

Shake well with ice and strain into glass. Fill with Soda Water.

Nicky's Fizz

2 Jiggers Dry Gin
1 Jigger Sweetened Grapefruit Juice

Shake well with ice and strain into glass. Fill up with Soda Water.

Orange Fizz No. 1

2 Jiggers Dry Gin
Juice of 1/2 Orange
1 Dash Grenadine

Shake well with ice and strain into glass. Fill up with Soda Water.

Orange Fizz No. 2

2 Jiggers Dry Gin
Juice of 1/2 Orange
Juice of 1/2 Lime
Juice of 1/4 Lemon

Shake well with ice and strain into glass. Fill up with Soda Water.

Ostend Fizz

1 Jigger Crème de Cassis
1 Jigger Kirsch

Shake well with ice and strain into glass. Fill up with Soda Water.

Peach Blow Fizz

2 Jiggers Dry Gin
2/3 Jigger Cream
1 Teaspoon Powdered Sugar
4 Mashed Strawberries
Juice of 1/2 Lemon
Juice of 1/2 Lime

Shake well with ice and strain into glass. Fill up with Soda Water.

Pineapple Fizz

2 Jiggers Light Rum
1/2 Tablespoon Powdered Sugar
2 Tablespoons Pineapple Juice
1 Dash Lime Juice

Shake well with ice and strain into glass. Fill up with Soda Water.

Note: Gin may be used instead of Rum if desired.

Ramoz Fizz

1-1/2 Jiggers Dry Gin
1 Egg White
2/3 Jigger Cream
3 Dashes Orange Flower Water
Juice of 1/2 Lime
Juice of 1/2 Lemon

Shake well with ice and pour into 10-ounce glass with the edge frosted with Lemon and Sugar. Add Soda Water if desired.

Rose in June Fizz

1 Jigger Gin
1 Jigger Framboise
Juice of 1 Orange
Juice of 2 Limes

Shake well with ice and strain into glass. Add several dashes of Soda Water.

Royal Fizz

1 Jigger Gin
1 Egg
1 Teaspoon Sugar
Juice of 1/2 Lemon

Shake well with ice and strain into glass. Fill up with Soda Water.

Ruby Fizz

2 Jiggers Sloe Gin
1 Egg White
1 Teaspoon Raspberry Syrup
Juice of 1/2 Lemon

Shake well with ice and strain into glass. Fill up with Soda Water.

Rum Fizz

1 Jigger Rum
1/2 Jigger Cherry Brandy
1/2 Teaspoon Sugar
Juice of 1/2 Lemon

Shake well with ice and strain into glass. Fill up with Soda Water.

Saratoga Fizz

1 Jigger Rye or Bourbon Whiskey
1/3 Jigger Lemon Juice
1 Teaspoon Lime Juice
1 Teaspoon Sugar
1 Egg White

Shake well with ice and pour into glass. Garnish with a Cherry.

Scotch Fizz

Make same as GIN FIZZ, using Scotch Whisky in place of Gin.

Seapea Fizz

2 Jiggers Pernod
Juice of 1/2 Lemon

Shake well with ice and strain into glass. Fill up with Soda Water.

Silver Ball Fizz

2 Jiggers Rhine Wine
2 Dashes Orange Flower Water
1 Teaspoon Powdered Sugar
1 Egg White
1 Jigger Grapefruit Juice

Shake well with ice and strain into glass. Fill up with Soda Water.

Silver Fizz

Make same as GIN FIZZ, adding White of 1 Egg.

Sloe Gin Fizz (see Bismarck Fizz)

Southside Fizz

Make same as GIN FIZZ, with Mint leaves added.

Strawberry Fizz

1 Jigger Gin
4 Crushed Strawberries
1/2 Teaspoon Sugar
Juice of 1/2 Lemon

Shake well with ice and strain into glass. Fill up with Soda Water.

Texas Fizz

1 Jigger Gin
1 Dash Grenadine
Juice of 1/4 Orange
Juice of 1/4 Lemon

Shake well with ice and strain into glass. Fill up with chilled Champagne.

Violet Fizz

1 Jigger Dry Gin
1 Teaspoon Raspberry Syrup
1 Teaspoon Cream
Juice of 1/2 Lemon

Shake well with ice and strain into glass. Fill up with Soda Water.

Applejack Flip (for 2)

2-2/3 Jiggers Applejack
1 Egg
2 Teaspoons Sugar
1/2 Cup Shaved Ice

Chill all ingredients and place in chilled container of electric blender. Cover and blend for 20 seconds. Pour into 6-ounce glasses and sprinkle with Nutmeg.

Blackberry Flip

2 Jiggers Blackberry Brandy
1 Egg
1 Teaspoon Powdered Sugar

Shake well with cracked ice and strain into glass. Sprinkle Nutmeg on top.

Boston Flip

Place in a shaker 1 Egg, 1 teaspoon Sugar, 1 jigger Madeira, and 1 jigger Rye Whiskey. Shake well with ice and strain into large cocktail glass. Sprinkle with Nutmeg.

Brandy Flip

Prepare same as BLACKBERRY FLIP.

Cherry Brandy Flip

Prepare same as BLACKBERRY FLIP.

Claret Flip (for 2)

1/3 Cup Claret
1 Egg
1 Teaspoon Sugar
1 Dash Angostura Bitters
1/2 Cup Shaved Ice

Follow directions for preparation of APPLEJACK FLIP.

Muscatel Flip (for 2)

1-1/3 Jiggers Brandy
1/4 Cup Muscatel Wine
1 Egg
1 Teaspoon Sugar
1 Tablespoon Cream
1/2 Cup Shaved Ice

Follow directions for preparation of APPLEJACK FLIP.

Port Flip

Prepare same as BLACKBERRY FLIP, adding 1 or 2 dashes Benedictine.

Rum Flip

Prepare same as BLACKBERRY FLIP.

Sherry Flip

Prepare same as BLACKBERRY FLIP.

Whiskey Flip

Prepare same as BLACKBERRY FLIP, adding 2 or 3 dashes Rum.

Whiskey Peppermint Flip

Make same as BLACKBERRY FLIP, adding 1/3 jigger Peppermint.

FLOATS

Brandy Float

Place 1 or 2 cubes of Ice in an Old-Fashioned glass and fill it nearly full of chilled Soda Water. Lay the bowl of a teaspoon just at the top and pour in Brandy carefully so that it flows out over the surface but does not mix. The amount of Brandy is optional.

Rum or any Whiskey may be substituted for the Brandy.

Liqueur Float

Fill a Liqueur glass almost full of any Liqueur you desire. Pour in Cream carefully so that it floats on top.

FRAPPÉS

Frappés may be made in three ways and of any Liquor or Liqueur—or combination—you desire.

1. Fill a cocktail glass with shaved Ice and pour in the Liquor. Serve with a straw.

2. Fill a shaker about half full of shaved Ice, add the Liquor, shake thoroughly and strain into glass.

3. Blend shaved Ice and Liquor or Liqueur together in an electric blender and pour unstrained into glass.

Ale Flip (for 4)

Place 1 quart of Ale in a saucepan on the fire and let it come to a boil. Have ready the Whites of 2 Eggs and the Yolks of 4, well beaten separately. Add them bit by bit to 4 tablespoons Sugar which has been moistened with a little Water and sprinkled with 1/2 teaspoon Nutmeg. When all are mixed, pour in the hot Ale, beating as you do so; and then pour from the original bowl into another one and backwards and forwards several times till the Flip is smooth and frothy.

Apple Toddy

Place 1/4 Baked Apple in a glass with 1 teaspoon Powdered Sugar and 2 jiggers Calvados or Applejack. Fill glass with boiling Water and serve with grating of Nutmeg.

Black Stripe

Place 1 teaspoon Molasses in a heated tumbler with 2 jiggers Dark Rum and a twist of Lemon Peel. Add boiling Water. Stir and serve.

Blue Blazer

This drink requires 2 good-sized mugs with handles. Put 2 jiggers Scotch Whisky in 1 mug and 2 jiggers boiling Water in the other. Blaze the Scotch and while it is blazing, pour the ingredients back and forth from 1 mug to the other. If you do this properly it will look like a stream of fire. Add 1 teaspoon Fine grain Sugar and serve in a heated tumbler with a twist of Lemon Peel.

Brandy Blazer

Combine in a small thick glass 2 jiggers Brandy, 1 lump

Sugar and 1 twist of Orange Peel. Blaze the Brandy and stir with a long spoon. Strain into cocktail glass and serve.

Brandy Toddy

Dissolve 1 lump of Sugar in a tumbler with a little Water and add 2 jiggers Brandy, a twist of Lemon Peel and fill with boiling Water. Stir and serve.

Café Brûlot

8 Lumps Sugar
6 Jiggers Cognac
2 Sticks Cinnamon, broken
1 Twist Lemon Peel
12 Whole Cloves
2 Large Twists Orange Peel
5 Demi-tasse Cups of Strong Black Coffee

Place all ingredients, except Coffee, in a Chafing-Dish. Heat gently, stirring constantly with a metal ladle, until well warmed. Blaze and let burn about 1 minute. Slowly pour in the black Coffee. Ladle into Demi-tasse cups and serve.

Café Brûlot Cocktail

Moisten the edge of a heavy glass with a piece of Lemon. Dip in Powdered Sugar and add about 3 jiggers hot Coffee. Float 2/3 jigger Brandy on top. Blaze and serve.

Café Diable

This is essentially the same as CAFÉ BRÛLOT but requires a longer blazing period.

Café Royale

Place a lump of Sugar in a spoon and balance over a Demi-tasse cup of hot black Coffee. Fill the spoon with Brandy and when warm, blaze. As the flame begins to fade pour the contents into the Coffee.

Christmas Punch No. 1

Combine in a large saucepan or heatproof dish 2 bottles of Brandy, 2 bottles Champagne, 1 pound of Sugar and 1 pound of cubed fresh Pineapple. Heat to a foam but do not boil. Pour

Brandy on top and blaze. Let burn for 1 minute and ladle into heated Wineglasses.

Columbia Skin

Heat in a small saucepan 1 tablespoon Water, 2 lumps of Sugar, the Juice of 1/2 Lemon, 1 teaspoon Curaçao and 2 jiggers Rum. Let foam but do not boil. Serve in heated Wineglass.

Note: Brandy, Gin or Whiskey may be prepared as above.

English Bishop (for about 6)

Stick an Orange generously with Cloves and sprinkle it with Brown Sugar. Place it in a medium hot oven until moderately browned. Quarter it and place it in a heavy saucepan with 1 quart of hot Port. Simmer about 20 minutes and ladle into heated Punch glasses. Add 1/2 jigger Brandy to each glass before serving.

Festival Punch (for about 10)

1 Quart Jamaica Rum
1 Quart Sweet Apple Cider
2 or 3 Sticks Cinnamon, broken
2 Teaspoons Ground Allspice
1 or 2 Tablespoons Butter

Heat ingredients in a heavy saucepan until almost boiling. Serve hot in mugs.

Glögg (for 12)

3/4 Cup Granulated Sugar
2/3 Jigger Angostura Bitters
6 Jiggers Claret
6 Jiggers Sherry
3 Jiggers Brandy

Heat all ingredients in a heavy saucepan. Place spoons in heated Old-Fashioned glasses and pour 3/4 full with the hot mixture.

Hot Benefactor

Place in a heated tumbler 2 lumps Sugar, dissolved with a little Boiling Water. Add 2 jiggers each Jamaica Rum and Burgundy. Fill with Boiling Water and serve with a slice of Lemon and a grating of Nutmeg.

Hot Buttered Rum

2 Jiggers Jamaica Rum
1 Twist Lemon Peel
1 Stick Cinnamon
1 or 2 Cloves
Boiling Cider
Butter

Place Rum, Lemon Peel, Clove and Cinnamon in a Pewter Tankard or heavy mug. Fill with Boiling Cider. Float a pat of Butter on top and stir well.

Hot Gin

2 Jiggers Gin
1 or 2 Lumps Sugar
Juice of 1/2 Lemon

Place in small tumbler and fill with hot Water. Serve with a spoon.

Hot Lemonade

This is made the same as LEMONADE (Plain) – see Index–using Hot Water instead of the chilled Soda. Frequently a jigger of Whiskey, Brandy or Rum is added.

Hot Locomotive

1 Egg Yolk
1-1/2 Teaspoons Sugar
2/3 Jigger Honey
4 Jiggers Burgundy or Claret
1/3 Jigger Curaçao

Blend Egg Yolk, Sugar and Honey in a small saucepan. Add Wine and Curaçao and heat to the simmering point. Pour back and forth several times into a heated mug. Serve with a thin Lemon slice and pinch of Cinnamon.

Hot Milk Punch

1 Jigger Light Rum
1 Jigger Brandy
1 Teaspoon Sugar
Hot Milk

Combine the Sugar, Rum and Brandy in a tall glass. Fill with Hot Milk. Stir and top with Nutmeg.

Hot Rum Bowl (for approximately 16)

1 Quart Jamaica Rum
3 Quarts Sweet Apple Cider
1 Cup Brown Sugar
1 Cup Boiling Water
Butter
Nutmeg

In a saucepan dissolve Sugar in Boiling Water. Add Cider and heat. Add Rum and 1 or 2 generous teaspoons

Butter. Place in a heated bowl and sprinkle with Nutmeg. Serve in mugs.

Hot Rum Lemonade

Combine 1 teaspoon Sugar, the Juice of 1/2 Lemon and 1 jigger Rum in a heated tumbler or mug. Add freshly Boiling Water and a slice of Lemon.

Hot Rye

In a small tumbler dissolve 1 lump Sugar in a very little hot Water. Add 1 small piece Cinnamon, 1 twist Lemon Peel and 2 jiggers Rye Whiskey. Serve hot Water in a pitcher on the side, to be added as desired.

Hot Scotch

Prepare same as HOT RYE.

Hot Toddies

2/3 Jigger Applejack, Brandy, Rum or any Whiskey
1 Teaspoon Sugar
2 Cloves
1 Slice Lemon

Place ingredients in Old-Fashioned glass with a silver spoon and fill with Boiling Water. A small piece of Cinnamon may be added if desired.

Hot Toddy Bowl (for about 16)

1 Quart Applejack, Brandy, Rum or any Whiskey
2 Quarts Boiling Water
1 Whole Lemon
Whole Cloves
Sugar Syrup to taste

Stud the Lemon with whole Cloves and slice it as thin as possible. Combine the Liquor, Sugar Syrup to taste and Lemon slices in a heated bowl. Add the Boiling Water and serve in hot mugs with a Lemon slice in each serving. Cinnamon may be added if desired.

Hot Wine Lemonade

1 Jigger Red Wine
Juice of 1/2 or 1 Lemon
1-1/2 Teaspoons Sugar
Twist of Lemon Peel

Combine Sugar, Juice and Wine in a hot tumbler or mug. Add Boiling Water and twist of Lemon Peel.

Jersey Flamer (for 8)

1 Quart Applejack
2/3 Jigger Angostura Bitters
1 Cup Sugar
2 Large Twists Lemon Peel
1 Quart Boiling Water

Combine in saucepan the Applejack, Bitters, Sugar and Lemon Peel. Heat slightly and stir to dissolve the Sugar. Turn into a heated heatproof bowl. Blaze and while blazing, pour on Boiling Water. Serve in heated mugs.

Jersey Mug

Place in a heated mug 2 jiggers Applejack, 1 good dash Angostura Bitters, several whole Cloves and a large twist of Lemon Peel. Fill with Boiling Water and float Applejack on top. Blaze and serve.

Mariner's Grog

1 Jigger Jamaica Rum
1 Lump Sugar
Several Cloves
1 Small Stick Cinnamon
Juice of 1/2 Lemon
1 Slice Lemon

Place all ingredients in a heavy mug. Fill with Boiling Water and stir and serve.

Mulled Wine

2-1/2 Jiggers Claret or any other Red Wine
5 Jiggers Water
1 Dash Angostura Bitters
1 Teaspoon Sugar
1 Large Twist Lemon Peel
1 Pinch Allspice
1 Small Piece Cinnamon
Several Cloves

Heat all together in a saucepan but do not boil. Place a Silver spoon in a large tumbler and strain in the mixture.

Note: MULLED CIDER may be prepared the same way, using 7 jiggers Cider instead of Wine and Water. A dash of Rum may be added.

Negus

Heat 1 bottle of Sherry or Port and place in a pitcher. Rub a little Lemon Rind on 6 cubes of Sugar and add to the mixture. Also add 2–3 large twists of Rind and the Juice of 1 Lemon. Add 10 drops of Vanilla and 2 cups of Boiling Water. Sweeten to taste if necessary and strain into glasses. Add a grating of Nutmeg and serve. Makes 8 cups.

Tom and Jerry

12 Eggs
6 Tablespoons Granulated Sugar
1 Teaspoon Grated Nutmeg
Rum
Bourbon or Rye
Hot Milk or Boiling Water

Beat the Eggs until thick and light in color. Gradually add the Sugar and Nutmeg and continue beating until the batter is very thick. Chill for several hours. To serve, put 1 heaping tablespoon of the batter into a warm mug. Add 1/2 jigger Rum and 1 jigger Bourbon or Rye. Fill the mug with hot milk or boiling water as desired. Stir and serve with a light grating of Nutmeg on top. More Liquor may be used if desired but in the same proportion as above.

Wassail

12 Eggs
4 Bottles Sherry or Madeira
2 Pounds Sugar
1 Teaspoon Powdered Nutmeg
2 Teaspoons Ginger
6 Whole Cloves
1/2 Teaspoon Mace
6 Whole Allspice
1 Teaspoon Cinnamon

Mix the dry ingredients in 1/2 pint of Water. Add the Wine and let the mixture simmer over a very slow fire. Beat the Egg Yolks and Whites separately and add these to the hot brew. Before serving, add several Baked Apples and lace the mixture well with Brandy. Makes 25 to 30 cups.

Whiskey Lemonade

Prepare same as HOT RUM LEMONADE, substituting Whiskey for Rum.

JULEPS

You will rarely find two people in any gathering who will agree as to what is or what is not a proper MINT JULEP. The recipe given is certainly an easy one to follow and is as good as they come.

Mint Julep

2 Jiggers Bourbon
1 Teaspoon Powdered Sugar
Mint
Soda Water

Fill a Collins glass with crushed ice and set it aside. Strip the leaves from 2 sprigs of Mint and muddle them in a small glass with the Sugar. Add a small splash of Soda Water, muddle again and add the Bourbon. Stir and strain into the prepared glass over the ice. Work a long-handled spoon up and down in the mixture until the outside of the glass begins to frost. Decorate with sprigs of Mint. Add more Whiskey if desired. Sometimes the Julep is topped with a splash of Rum.

Note: This same Julep may be made with Applejack, Brandy, Gin, Rum or Rye Whiskey. A CHAMPAGNE JULEP is also delicious but when making one, more Champagne will be needed and perhaps a dash of Brandy added. The GIN MINT JULEP is frequently called a MAJOR BAILEY and may be served as a cocktail.

Americano

Place in a tumbler 2 jiggers Sweet Vermouth and 1 jigger Campari. Add 2 ice cubes and a twist of Lemon Peel. Fill with Soda Water.

American Punch

2/3 Jigger Brandy
2/3 Jigger Dry Vermouth
1 Teaspoon Crème de Menthe
Juice of 1/2 Orange
1/2 Teaspoon Sugar

Shake Juice, Sugar, Brandy and Vermouth with cracked ice. Strain into 10-ounce glass or large goblet filled with shaved ice and the Crème de Menthe.

American Rose

1 Jigger Brandy
1 Dash Pernod
1 Teaspoon Grenadine
2 Slices of Ripe Peach, crushed with a fork

Shake in a shaker with crushed ice and strain into 10-ounce glass. Fill with chilled Champagne.

Angostura Highball

Place in a tumbler 2 cubes of ice, 1 teaspoon Angostura Bitters and fill up with Ginger Ale.

Bermuda Highball

3/4 Jigger Dry Gin
3/4 Jigger Brandy
1/2 Jigger Dry Vermouth

Combine ingredients in highball glass, with ice cubes, and fill with Ginger Ale or Soda Water. Garnish with Lemon Peel and serve.

Bishop

Fill a tumbler 1/2 full with cracked ice. Add 1 teaspoon Sugar, Juice of 1/2 Lemon, Juice of 1/2 Orange and fill with Burgundy or Claret. Stir and add 1 slice of Orange and several dashes of Rum.

Black Rose

In a tumbler or highball glass, with 2 cubes of ice, place 1 teaspoon Sugar, 1 jigger St. James Rum and fill with cold black Coffee. Stir and serve.

Byrrh Cassis

Combine in a tumbler or highball glass, with 2 cubes of ice, 1 teaspoon Crème de Cassis and 2 jiggers Byrrh. Fill with Soda Water, stir and serve.

California Lemonade

1 Jigger Rye Whiskey
1 Dash Grenadine
Juice of 1 Lemon
Juice of 1 Lime
1 Tablespoon Powdered Sugar

Shake well with ice and strain into glass. Fill with chilled Soda Water.

Cassisco

Place 2 cubes of ice in a tumbler or large goblet. Add 1 tablespoon Crème de Cassis and 1 jigger Brandy. Fill with Soda Water and serve.

Cincinnati

Fill a highball glass 1/2 full of Beer. Fill up with chilled Soda Water and serve.

Cloak and Dagger

Fill a highball glass with ice cubes. Add 1-1/2 jiggers Jamaica Rum and fill with Cola. Add a generous twist of Orange Peel and a dash of Orange Bitters.

Cocoa Rickey

Place a scoop of Vanilla Ice Cream in a large highball glass. Add 1 jigger Crème de Cacao, 1 tablespoon Milk and fill with Soda Water. Stir and add Sugar if necessary.

Corpse Reviver No. 3

Place 1 or 2 ice cubes in a highball glass and add the Juice of 1/4 Lemon, 1 jigger Pernod and fill with chilled Champagne. Stir and serve.

Cuba Libre

Place 2 or 3 ice cubes in a large highball glass. Add 2 jiggers Rum, the Juice of 1/2 Lime and fill with Cola.

Doctor Funk

1-2/3 Jiggers Martinique Rum
1/8 Jigger Pernod
1/3 Jigger Lemon Juice
1/8 Jigger Grenadine
1/4 Teaspoon Sugar
1 Lime

Cut Lime in half and squeeze into shaker, dropping in the Rinds also. Add all other ingredients and shake with crushed ice. Pour into 12-ounce glass and if necessary fill with Soda Water. Decorate with fruit if desired.

Dog's Nose

Place 1 or 2 jiggers Gin in a tall highball glass. Fill up with cold Beer or Stout.

El Diabolo

1 Jigger Tequila
1/3 Jigger Crème de Cassis
1/2 Lime
Ginger Ale

Squeeze and drop the Lime into highball glass. Add ice and other ingredients and fill with Ginger Ale.

Florida Special No. 2

2 Jiggers Gin
Juice of 1/2 Orange
Rind of Whole Orange, cut in spiral form

Place Orange Rind in tall glass and add ice and other ingredients. Fill with Ginger Ale.

Fog Cutter

1-1/3 Jiggers Puerto Rican Rum
2/3 Jigger Brandy
1/3 Jigger Gin
2/3 Jigger Orange Juice
1 Jigger Lemon Juice
1/3 Jigger Orgeat Syrup
Sherry

Shake all the ingredients, except the Sherry, with cracked ice and pour into a 14-ounce glass with the ice. Float the Sherry on top and serve with straws.

Fog Horn

Place 2 cubes of ice in a highball glass. Add 2 jiggers Dry Gin and 1 slice of Lemon. Fill with Ginger Beer and serve.

Frank's Refresher

Combine in a tumbler or highball glass, with 2 cubes of ice, the Juice of 1/2 Lemon, 1 jigger Raspberry Syrup and 1 jigger Brandy. Fill with chilled Champagne and serve.

Gin and Tonic

Place 2 jiggers Dry Gin in a highball glass with 2 or 3 cubes of ice and 1 slice of Lemon. Fill with Tonic Water.

Gin Buck

Place the Juice of 1/2 Lime and 2 twists of Lime Peel in a highball glass with 2 jiggers Gin and ice cubes. Fill up with Ginger Ale.

Golden Lemonade

1 Jigger Eau de Vie de Danzig
1 Jigger Amer Picon
1 Egg Yolk
1 Tablespoon Powdered Sugar
Juice of 2 Limes

Shake well with cracked ice and strain into glass. Fill with chilled Soda Water.

Highballs

Place in a 10-ounce glass ice cubes and 1 or 2 jiggers of any of the liquors listed below. Fill up with Soda Water or plain Water and, if desired, garnish with twist of Lemon Peel.

Applejack
Bourbon
Brandy
Gin
Irish Whiskey
Rum
Rye Whiskey
Scotch Whisky

Note: Occasionally such Wines as Dubonnet, etc. are used to make highballs in the same manner.

Horse's Neck

1 or 2 Jiggers Whiskey
Rind of 1 Lemon
Ginger Ale

Cut Rind in spiral and place in tall highball glass. Add Whiskey and ice cubes and fill up with Ginger Ale.

Lemonade (Plain)

Juice of 1/2 Lemon
Juice of 1/2 Lime
2 Tablespoons Powdered Sugar

Shake well with ice and strain into tall glass. Add extra ice if desired and fill with chilled Soda Water. All Lemon Juice or all Lime Juice may be used instead of half and half. And to vary the drink, Grenadine or other similar sweetening may be used instead of Sugar. Sometimes an Egg is shaken with the mixture. Or, again, the Plain Lemonade is occasionally served with a Claret Float. (See Floats.)

Macka

Fill a tumbler or highball glass 1/2 full with cracked ice. Add 1 dash Crème de Cassis and 1/3 each Gin and Sweet and Dry Vermouth. Stir well. Add slice of Orange and serve.

Major Bailey (see Juleps)

Mamie Taylor

In a large tumbler or highball glass, with ice cubes, place 1 slice of Lemon, 2 jiggers Gin or Scotch Whisky and fill with Ginger Ale. Stir and serve.

Modern Lemonade

1 Jigger Sherry
1 Jigger Sloe Gin
2 Tablespoons Powdered Sugar
Juice of 1 Lemon

Stir well with ice and strain into glass. Add twist of Lemon Peel and fill with chilled Soda Water.

Mojito

1-1/3 Jiggers Puerto Rican Rum
1/2 Lime
1 Teaspoon Sugar
Mint Leaves

Squeeze Lime into 10-ounce glass and drop in Rind. Add other ingredients and fill 2/3 full with shaved ice. Add Soda Water, stir and serve.

Moscow Mule

Squeeze into a 12-ounce glass 1/2 Lime and drop in the Rind. Add ice cubes and 1-1/2 jiggers Vodka and fill with Ginger Beer. Stir and serve.

O'Hearn Special

2 Jiggers Brandy
1 Twist Orange Peel
2 Sprigs Mint

Place in tall glass with ice cubes. Fill up with Ginger Ale. Stir and serve.

Pineapple Lemonade

1 Jigger Brandy
1 Dash Raspberry Syrup
1 Teaspoon Powdered Sugar
2 Slices Pineapple

Muddle the Pineapple and Sugar well in a shaker. Add other ingredients and shake well with ice. Strain into glass and decorate with twist of Lemon Peel and Pineapple Stick if desired.

Pompier

2 Jiggers French Vermouth
2/3 Jigger Crème de Cassis

Place in highball glass with ice cubes and fill up with Soda Water.

Shandy Gaff

Fill tall glass half and half with chilled Ale and Ginger Ale.

Spritzer

Place 2 jiggers White Wine in highball glass with ice cubes and fill with Soda Water.

Stone Fence No. 2

2 Jiggers Scotch Whisky
1/2 Teaspoon Sugar
1 Cube of Ice

Place in tumbler or highball glass and fill with chilled Soda Water. Stir and serve.

Swedish Highball

2 Jiggers Swedish Punch
1 Dash Bitters

Place in highball glass with ice cubes and fill up with chilled Soda Water.

Tomate

Place in a tumbler or highball glass with ice cubes 2 dashes Pernod and 1 teaspoon Grenadine. Fill with plain Water as desired.

Vermouth Cassis (see Pompier)

Zombie

2/3 Jigger Rum, 90 proof
1-1/3 Jiggers Gold Seal Rum, 86 proof
2/3 Jigger White Label Rum, 86 proof
2/3 Jigger Pineapple Juice
2/3 Jigger Papaya Juice, if available
Juice of 1 Lime
1 Teaspoon Powdered Sugar

Shake well with ice and pour into 14-ounce glass. Decorate with Pineapple and Cherry and float on top Demerara Rum, 151 proof. Sprinkle lightly with Powdered Sugar and serve.

PUFFS

All Puffs are served in small tumblers.

Brandy Puff

Place 1 or 2 ice cubes in a glass and add 1 or 2 jiggers Brandy and 1 or 2 jiggers Milk. Fill with chilled Soda Water, stir gently and serve.

Note: The GIN, RUM or WHISKEY PUFF is made the same as above, substituting the desired liquor.

American Punch

2 Jiggers White Crème de Menthe
1 Jigger Crème d'Yvette
1 Dash Grenadine
1 Tablespoon Powdered Sugar
Juice of 1 Lemon

Place Sugar and Lemon Juice in bottom of tall glass and dissolve with a little Soda Water. Add Grenadine and fill with cracked ice. Float Liqueurs on top, keeping them separate. Decorate with fruit as desired. Serves 1.

Applejack Punch

2 Quarts Applejack
4 Jiggers Grenadine
1 Pint Orange Juice

Combine the ingredients in a punch bowl with a block of ice. Just before serving add 2 quarts chilled Ginger Ale. Decorate with fruit if desired. Makes 25 to 30 cups.

Artillery Punch

1 Quart Strong Black Tea
1 Quart Rye Whiskey
1 Bottle Red Wine
1 Pint Jamaica Rum
1/2 Pint Dry Gin
1/2 Pint Brandy
1 Jigger Benedictine
1 Pint Orange Juice
1/2 Pint Lemon Juice

Combine all ingredients in a large punch bowl with a block of ice. If found too dry, Sugar Syrup may be added. Decorate with twists of Lemon Peel. Makes 25 to 30 cups.

Bacardi Punch

Fill a tall glass with shaved ice. Pour in 1/2 jigger Grenadine and 2 jiggers Bacardi Rum. Stir until glass is frosted and decorate with fruit. Serves 1.

Baccio (for 8)

Combine in a large punch

bowl with a block of ice 5 jiggers Grapefruit Juice, 5 jiggers Dry Gin, 2 jiggers Anisette and slices of Orange and Lemon. Add a little Sugar Syrup to taste. Just before serving pour in 1 split chilled Soda Water and 1 split chilled Champagne. Stir slightly.

Baltimore Eggnog

Separate the Whites and Yolks of 12 Eggs. Beat with the Egg Yolks 1 pound Powdered Sugar. Stir in slowly 1 pint Brandy, 1/2 pint Light Rum, 1/2 pint Peach Brandy, 3 pints Milk and 1 pint Heavy Cream. Chill thoroughly and fold in stiffly beaten Egg Whites before serving. Makes 25 to 30 cups.

Basic Eggnog (for 1)

Combine in a shaker with ice 2 jiggers Brandy or Light Rum, 1 Egg, 1 tablespoon Sugar and 3/4 cup Milk. Shake well and strain into glass. Sprinkle with Nutmeg.

Best Punch

1 Cup Strong Tea
Juice of 2 Lemons
1 Teaspoon Sugar
2 Jiggers Brandy
1 Jigger Curaçao
1 Jigger Medford Rum

Place a large block of ice in a punch bowl. Add the above ingredients. Just before serving, add 1 quart chilled Soda Water and 1 quart chilled Champagne. Makes 10 to 12 cups.

Bombay Punch (2 gallons)

Combine in a mixing bowl, without ice, 1 quart Brandy, 1 quart Sherry, 1/4 pint Maraschino, 1/2 Orange Curaçao and 2 quarts chilled Soda Water. Set punch bowl in a bed of crushed ice, decorate with fruits as desired, and just before serving add 4 quarts chilled Champagne.

Bourbon Eggnog (for 12)

Beat Yolks and Whites of 8 Eggs separately, adding 1/2 pound Sugar to the Whites. Combine beaten Yolks and Whites and blend gently. Stir in 2 jiggers Rum and 1 bottle Bourbon, 1 pint heavy Cream and 1 quart Milk. Mix all together and chill thoroughly. Serve with grated Nutmeg on top.

Brandy Eggnog

Prepare same as BOURBON EGGNOG, using Brandy.

Brandy Punch

(As served by Patrick Gavin Duffy to the members of the Sothern Company during rehearsals at the old Lyceum Theatre.)

Juice of 15 Lemons
Juice of 4 Oranges
1-1/4 Pounds Powdered Sugar
1/2 Pint Curaçao
1 or 2 Jiggers Grenadine
2 Quarts Brandy

Place in punch bowl with large block of ice and just before serving add 1 or 2 quarts Soda Water. Makes 25 to 30 cups.

Breakfast Eggnog

1 Fresh Egg
3/4 Brandy
1/4 Curaçao
1/4 Milk

Shake well with ice and strain into tall glass. Grate Nutmeg on top.

Bride's Bowl (for 20)

Dice 2 cups Fresh Pineapple and place in a punch bowl with 1/2 cup Sugar Syrup, 1 cup Lemon Juice, 1-1/2 cups Unsweetened Pineapple Juice, 1-1/3 cups Peach Brandy and 1-1/2 or 2 bottles Medium Rum. Add block of ice and before serving pour in 2 quarts chilled Soda Water and 1 pint sliced Strawberries.

Buddha Punch (for 10)

1/4 Quart Rhine Wine
4 Jiggers Orange Juice
4 Jiggers Lemon Juice
2 Jiggers Curaçao
2 Jiggers Medium Rum
1 Dash Angostura Bitters

Combine in punch bowl with block of ice and just before serving add 1 bottle chilled Soda Water and 1 bottle chilled Champagne. Garnish with twists of Lemon Peel and Mint leaves.

Burgundy Punch (for 15)

Combine in a punch bowl with a block of ice 2 quarts Burgundy, 5 jiggers Port, 3 jiggers Cherry Brandy, Juice of 3 Lemons, Juice of 6 Oranges, 1 or 2 tablespoons Sugar and a long twist each Lemon and Orange Peel. Just before serving add 2 bottles chilled Soda Water.

Cardinal (1-1/2 gallons)

Place 1-1/2 pounds Sugar in a punch bowl and dissolve with 2 quarts Soda Water. Add 2 quarts Claret, 1 pint Brandy, 1 pint Rum, 1 jigger Sweet Vermouth, 1 sliced Orange and 2 or 3 slices Fresh Pineapple. Stir and add block of ice. Just before serving add 1 pint of any Sparkling White Wine.

Christmas Punch No. 2 (50 drinks)

In a large punch bowl combine 1 quart strong Tea with a bottle each Rum, Rye Whiskey and Brandy, 1/2 bottle Benedictine, 1 tablespoon Angostura Bitters and 1 sliced Pineapple. Add the Juice of 12 Oranges, 1/2 or 1 pound Sugar, dissolved in Water, and mix together thoroughly. Add block of ice and just before serving pour in 2 quarts of chilled Champagne.

Claret Punch No. 1

Fill a tall glass 1/2 full of cracked ice. Add 1 teaspoon each Lemon Juice, Grenadine and Curaçao. Fill with Claret or Burgundy and decorate with slice of Orange. Serve with a straw.

Claret Punch No. 2

Mix together 2 bottles Claret, 1/4 pound Sugar, the Rind of 1 Lemon and chill for several hours. Place block of ice in a punch bowl, pour in the iced mixture. Add 1-1/2 jiggers Cognac, 1-1/2 jiggers Curaçao and 1-1/2 jiggers Sherry. Before serving pour in 2 bottles chilled Soda Water. Makes 25 to 30 cups.

Colonial Tea Punch

Remove the Peel in thin strips from 12 Lemons and place the strips in a punch bowl. Add 1 quart strong Tea and the Juice from the Lemons. Mix with 2 cups Sugar and let stand for 1 hour. Add 1 quart Dark Rum and 1 jigger Brandy. Pour the mixture over crushed ice and serve. Makes 12 to 15 cups.

Curaçao Punch

Place in a large glass 1/2 teaspoon Sugar, the Juice of 1/2 Lemon, 1 jigger Curaçao and 1 jigger Brandy or Rum. Fill with shaved ice and stir lightly. Decorate with fruit if desired and serve with a straw.

Dragoon (see Champagne)

Dubonnet Party Punch

Pour 1 bottle Dubonnet into a large pitcher and add 1 pint Gin, the Juice and Rind of 6 Limes and 1 bottle of chilled Soda Water. Fill tall glasses with crushed ice and decorate with Mint. Pour in the Punch. Makes 15 to 20 glasses.

Fish House Punch No. 1 (for 25)

Dissolve 3/4 pound Sugar in a large punch bowl with a little Water. When entirely dissolved stir in 1 quart Lemon Juice, 2 quarts Jamaica Rum, 2 quarts Water and add Peach Brandy to taste. Place 1 large block of ice in punch bowl and allow mixture to chill 2 hours. Serve in punch or cocktail glasses.

Fish House Punch No. 2 (the best)

Dissolve in a punch bowl 1-1/2 cups Sugar in 1 cup Water and 3 cups Lemon Juice. Add 3 pints Dry White Wine, 1 bottle Jamaica Rum, 1 bottle Gold Label Rum, 1 bottle Cognac and 2-1/2 jiggers Peach Brandy. Let the mixture stand for 2 or 3 hours, stirring it occasionally. Before serving add a block of ice, stir to cool and serve. If a stronger Punch is desired do not add the block of ice to the punch bowl but set the bowl in a bed of crushed ice to chill.

Gin Punch No. 1

Place in a tall glass 1 lump Sugar, 1 twist Lemon Peel, Juice of 1/2 Lemon, 2 dashes Maraschino and 2 jiggers Dry Gin. Add cracked ice and fill with Soda Water. Stir and serve.

Gin Punch No. 2 (for 12)

Combine the Juice of 12 Lemons, the Juice of 20 Oranges, 2 quarts Gin, 4 jiggers Grenadine. Pour over large block of ice. Add 2 bottles chilled Soda Water. Decorate with fruit as desired and serve.

Instant Eggnog

Place 2 quarts French Vanilla Ice Cream in a punch bowl. Add 1 bottle Bourbon and 2 jiggers Jamaica Rum. Stir until creamy and sprinkle with Nutmeg.

Ladies' Punch

Combine in a shaker 2 tablespoons Powdered Sugar, 1 Egg, 1/2 jigger Maraschino, 1 jigger Crème de Cacao, 1 twist Orange Peel, 1 cup Milk, 2 dashes Nutmeg. Shake well with ice and strain into glass. Serve with additional Nutmeg on top.

Milk Punch (Basic)

Note: The following recipe may be used for Applejack, Bourbon, Brandy, Rum, Rye or Scotch Whisky.

Combine in a shaker with cracked ice 1 or 2 jiggers any liquor desired and 1 cup Milk, 1 tablespoon Powdered Sugar. Shake well and strain into glass. Sprinkle each serving with Nutmeg.

Myrtle Bank Punch

Combine in shaker with a large piece of ice 1 jigger Demerara Rum, 151 Proof, Juice of 1/2 Lime, 6 dashes Grenadine and 1 teaspoon Sugar. Shake and pour over cracked ice in a 10-ounce glass. Float Maraschino Liqueur on top.

Navy Punch (for 10)

Slice 4 Pineapples and sprinkle well with 1 pound fine Sugar. Add 1/2 bottle Dark Rum, 1/2 bottle Cognac, 1/2 bottle Peach Brandy and the Juice of 4 Lemons. Chill well. Pour into punch bowl with block of ice. Decorate with fruit as desired and add 4 quarts of chilled Champagne.

Nourmahal Punch

Squeeze 1/2 Lime and drop it into a 10-ounce glass with cracked ice. Add 2 jiggers Redheart Rum, 2 dashes Angostura Bitters and fill with Soda Water.

Nuremburg (for 15)

Place 3/4 pound lump Sugar in a large bowl and strain over it through a fine sieve the Juice of 2 or 3 large Oranges. Add twists of the Peel cut very thin and pour in 1 quart boiling Water, 1/3 Quart Arrack, 1 bottle of Red Wine, which has been heated but not boiled. Stir all together and let cool. Pour into tall glasses over cracked ice.

Note: The mixed ingredients may be bottled. They improve with age.

Patrick Gavin Duffy's Punch

Combine in a shaker with ice 2 jiggers Brandy, 1 jigger Benedictine, 1/2 teaspoon Powdered Sugar, Juice of 1 Orange. Shake well and pour into tall glass. Decorate with Mint and fruit if desired. Serve with a straw.

Pendennis Eggnog

Mix together 1 pound Powdered Sugar and 1 bottle Bourbon. Let stand for 2 hours. Separate 12 Eggs and beat the Yolks to a froth, adding the Sweetened Whiskey slowly. Let this stand for 2 hours. Whip 2 quarts Heavy Cream until stiff and whip the Egg Whites. Fold these separately into the Whiskey mixture and chill. This is one of the richest of all Eggnogs.

Pineapple Punch (for 10)

1-1/2 Quarts Moselle Wine
Juice of 3 Lemons
5 Dashes Angostura Bitters
2-1/2 Jiggers English Gin
2/3 Jigger Pine Syrup
2/3 Jigger Grenadine
2/3 Jigger Maraschino

Pour all together into punch bowl with 1 quart chilled Soda Water. Set bowl in bed of crushed ice to chill. Decorate with Pineapple.

Pisco Punch

In a large Wineglass or small tumbler place 1 piece of ice with a teaspoon each of Pineapple and Lemon Juice. Add 2 jiggers Brandy, a small cube of Pineapple and fill with cold Water. Stir well and serve.

Plantation Punch

Combine in a large Old-Fashioned glass 1 jigger Southern Comfort, 1/2 jigger Lemon Juice, 1/2 jigger Rum, 1 teaspoon Sugar. Fill with ice and a little Soda Water. Garnish with twist of Orange Peel and serve.

Planter's Punch

Using a tall glass with cracked ice as desired, pour in 1 part Lime Juice, 2 parts Sugar Syrup, 3 parts Jamaica Rum, 4 parts Water. This may be served with a Maraschino Cherry and a slice of Orange. The ice and water should be figured together as the 4 parts.

Quintet

3 Jiggers Brandy
3 Jiggers Dark Rum
4 Bottles White Wine
Juice of 8 Lemons
Juice of 8 Oranges

Combine in punch bowl with block of ice and fruit garnish as desired. Just before serving pour in 4 bottles chilled Soda Water. Serves 50 to 60.

Regent Punch (for 10)

2-1/2 Jiggers Brandy
2-1/2 Jiggers Swedish Punch
1-1/4 Jiggers Curaçao

1 Pint Jamaica Rum
Juice of 6 Lemons
1 Cup Strong Tea
1 Teaspoon Angostura Bitters
1-1/2 Quarts Champagne

Combine all the ingredients except the Champagne in a punch bowl set in a bed of crushed ice. Just before serving, pour in the Champagne and garnish with fruit as desired.

Rhine Wine Punch

3 Quarts Rhine Wine
1 Quart Chilled Soda Water
2-1/2 Jiggers Brandy
2-1/2 Jiggers Maraschino
1 Cup Strong Tea
1/2 Pound Powdered Sugar

Combine all the ingredients in a punch bowl set in a bed of crushed ice. Decorate with fruit as desired and serve when thoroughly chilled. Makes 25 to 30 cups.

Roman Punch (for 10)

2-1/2 Jiggers Brandy
2-1/2 Jiggers Swedish Punch
1-1/4 Jiggers Curaçao
1 Pint Jamaica Rum
Juice of 6 Lemons
1-1/2 Quarts Chilled Champagne
1 Teaspoon Angostura or Orange Bitters
1 Cup Strong Tea

Combine all the ingredients in a punch bowl set in a bed of crushed ice. Garnish with fruit as desired and serve when thoroughly chilled. Framboise may be used instead of the Curaçao.

Rum Cow

1 Jigger Puerto Rican Rum
2 Drops Vanilla
1 Pinch Nutmeg
1 Dash Angostura Bitters
1 Cup Milk
2 Teaspoons Sugar

Shake well with ice and pour into a tall glass. This is a specific for morning qualms.

Rum Eggnog

Prepare same as BRANDY EGGNOG, using Jamaica Rum.

Rum Punch (for a large party)

10 Bottles White Wine
2 Pounds Brown Sugar
2 Quarts Orange Juice
1 Quart Lemon Juice
10 Sliced Bananas
2 Fresh Pineapples, cut or chopped

Place the Fruit Juice, Rinds, Bananas, Pineapple and Wine in a crock with the Sugar. Cover and let stand overnight. In the morning add 6 bottles Light Rum and 1 bottle Jamaica Rum and 1 bottle Crème de Banane. Let stand until just before the party. Strain into punch bowl with ice as needed. Taste for seasoning and add either Sugar Syrup or Lemon Juice as you desire.

Rye Whiskey Punch

Shake with plenty of chopped ice 1 teaspoon Lemon Juice, 2 teaspoons Sugar and 2 jiggers Rye Whiskey. Pour unstrained into 10-ounce glass and decorate with slice of Orange.

Sauterne Punch

Fill a 10-ounce glass 1/2 full of cracked ice. Add 1/2 teaspoon Sugar, Juice of 1/2 Lemon, 1 or 2 teaspoons Curaçao and fill with Sauterne. Stir and decorate with fruit as desired. Serve with a straw.

Sauterne Punch No. 2 (for 10)

1/2 Pound Powdered Sugar
2 or 3 Quarts Sauterne
2-1/2 Jiggers Maraschino
2-1/2 Jiggers Curaçao
2-1/2 Jiggers Grand Marnier

Combine all together in a punch bowl with a large block of ice. Add several long twists of Lemon and Orange Peel and Mint if desired. Serve when well chilled.

Scotch Whisky Punch (for 12)

Combine in a pitcher with cracked ice 1 quart Scotch Whisky, the Juice and Rind of 3 Lemons, 1/2 cup Sugar and 1 quart Soda Water. Stir and pour into goblets with extra ice and garnish with fruit as desired.

Strawberry Punch

Place 1/2 teaspoon Sugar in a 10-ounce glass. Add a little Water to dissolve, and the Juice of 1/2 Lemon and 1 or 2 teaspoons Strawberry Syrup. Fill 2/3 with shaved ice and pour in 2 jiggers Brandy. Stir and decorate with Strawberries. Serve with a spoon and straw.

Whiskey Punch

Place a block of ice in a punch bowl and pour over it the Juice of 6 Lemons, the Juice of 8 Oranges, 2 tablespoons Sugar and 2 jiggers Curaçao. Stir and pour in 1-1/2 or 2 bottles of Rye, Bourbon or Blended Whiskey. Add fruits as desired and 2 quarts chilled Soda Water. Stir and serve.

Note: 1 quart of iced Tea may be substituted for 1 quart of Soda Water.

Xalapa Punch

Place the grated Peel of 2 Lemons in a punch bowl and pour over it 2-1/2 quarts strong hot Black Tea. Let this stand for 10 or 15 minutes and add 1 pint Sugar Syrup. Let cool. When cold add 1 bottle Applejack, 1 bottle Cuban Rum and 1 bottle Red Wine. Just before serving add a block of ice and 1 Lemon, sliced thin. Serve when well chilled.

Young People's Punch

Combine in a punch bowl 1/2 pint Sugar Syrup, 1/2 pint Lemon Juice, 1 pint Orange Juice, 2-1/2 jiggers Curaçao, 2-1/2 jiggers Pineapple Juice, 1-1/2 jiggers Maraschino and 2 bottles Red Wine. Chill with a block of ice and just before serving add 2 quarts of Soda Water. This Punch is excellent when spiked with Brandy as your judgment dictates.

Basic Rickey

Most Rickeys are made by the following recipe, using 1 or 2 jiggers of Applejack, Bourbon, Gin, Rum, or Whiskey as desired:

Place 1 cube of ice in a medium tumbler and add 1/2 Lime or 1/4 Lemon lightly squeezed. Pour in the amount and type of liquor desired and fill with chilled Soda Water. Serve with the Lime or Lemon rind in the glass.

Hugo Rickey

Make the same as GIN RICKEY with 2 dashes Grenadine and 1 slice Pineapple added.

Porto Rico Rickey

Make the same as GIN RICKEY with 2 dashes Raspberry Syrup added.

Savoy Hotel Rickey

Make the same as GIN RICKEY with 4 dashes Grenadine added.

SANGAREES

A Sangaree is always served in a tumbler which may be either small or large, depending on the ingredients used. Regardless of size, it will always have a grating of Nutmeg.

Ale, Porter or Stout Sangaree

Place in a large tumbler 1/2 teaspoon Sugar dissolved in a little Water. Fill with chilled Ale, Porter or Stout, stir very slightly and serve with a sprinkling of Nutmeg.

Brandy Sangaree

Place in a small tumbler 1/2 teaspoon Sugar dissolved in a little Water. Add 1 jigger Brandy and ice. Stir and serve with a sprinkling of Nutmeg.

Note: GIN, PORT, RUM, SHERRY and WHISKEY SANGAREES are all made in this same manner.

SCAFFAS

SCAFFAS are served unchilled, undiluted, in cocktail glasses.

Brandy Scaffa

Place in a cocktail glass 1 dash Angostura Bitters and 1/2 each Maraschino and Brandy. Stir and serve.

Gin Scaffa

Place in a cocktail glass 1 dash Angostura Bitters and 1/2 each Benedictine and Gin. Stir and serve.

Rum Scaffa

Place in a cocktail glass 1 dash Angostura Bitters and 1/2 each Benedictine and Rum. Stir and serve.

Whiskey Scaffa

Place in a cocktail glass 1 dash Angostura Bitters and 1/2 each Benedictine and Bourbon or Rye Whiskey. (A blend will do.) Stir and serve.

SHRUBS

Shrubs may be served either hot or cold but almost always from a large pitcher. And when cold, with plenty of Ice and a fruit garnish.

Brandy Shrub

To the thin Peels of 2 Lemons and the juice of 5, add 2 quarts of Brandy. Cover and let stand for 3 days, then add 1 quart Sherry and 2 pounds loaf Sugar. Stir well and strain through a fine sieve. Bottle and cork tightly.

Currant Shrub

Boil gently for 10 minutes 2 cups Sugar with 1 pint of strained Currant Juice, skimming frequently. Let cool and when lukewarm add 1 cup Brandy for each pint of the Shrub. Bottle and cork tightly.

Rum Shrub

Combine in a crock 3 pints Orange Juice and 1 pound Loaf Sugar to each 4 quarts of Rum. Cover well and leave for 6 weeks. Then strain, bottle and cork tightly.

White Currant Shrub

Combine 2 quarts of strained White Currant Juice with 4 quarts Rum and 2 pounds Loaf Sugar. Stir till the Sugar is dissolved, cover and let stand for several days. Strain and bottle. Cork tightly.

Brandy Sling

Place in a highball glass 3 cubes of Ice, 1 dash Angostura Bitters, the juice of 1/2 Lemon, 1 teaspoon Sugar and 2 jiggers Brandy. Fill with plain Water, stir well and serve.

Gin Sling

Place 1 teaspoon Sugar in a highball glass with 2 jiggers Dry Gin and several cubes of Ice. Fill with Water, stir well and serve. Soda may also be used.

Note: GIN SLINGS may be served hot; if so, sprinkle with a little Nutmeg.

Singapore Gin Sling

Combine in a shaker 1-1/3 jiggers Dry Gin, 2/3 jigger Cherry Brandy, 1 teaspoon Sugar, juice of 1/2 Lemon and 1 dash Angostura Bitters. Shake well with ice and strain into a tall glass. Add Ice and Soda as desired. Twist Lemon Peel over top and garnish with Fruit or Mint as desired. A dash of Benedictine may be added.

Straits Sling (for 6)

8 Jiggers Dry Gin
2 Jiggers Benedictine
2 Jiggers Cherry Brandy
Juice of 2 Lemons
1 Teaspoon Angostura Bitters
1 Teaspoon Orange Bitters

Shake well with Ice and strain into glasses. Fill with chilled Soda Water as desired and garnish with Fruit.

Vodka Sling

Prepare same as GIN SLING above.

SMASHES

SMASHES are nothing more than junior-size Juleps. They are served in small tumblers, or Old-Fashioned glasses.

Basic Recipe

Place 1 scant teaspoon fine grain Sugar in a glass with 2 sprigs fresh Mint and a few drops of Water. Crush the Mint with a muddler and fill glass half full of shaved ice. Pour in 1 or 2 jiggers of the desired liquor and if wanted a squirt of Soda Water. Decorate with Mint and serve.

Note: Brandy, Gin, Rum or any Whiskey may be used for this.

TODDIES

TODDIES, when served cold, are all made the same way whether Applejack, Brandy, Gin, Rum or any Whiskey is used.

Place in a small tumbler or Old-Fashioned glass 1 scant teaspoon Sugar. Dissolve with a little Water and leave the spoon in glass. Add 1 or 2 cubes of Ice and 2 jiggers of the desired Liquor. Stir and serve.

ZOOMS

Rum Zoom

Dissolve in a cup 1 teaspoon Honey in a little boiling Water. Pour into a shaker with 1 teaspoon Cream and 2 jiggers Rum. Add ice and shake well and strain into glass.

Note: BRANDY, GIN and WHISKEY ZOOMS are all made as above.

BUYING AND SERVING WINE

Wine is old as civilization. The ancient Babylonians were wine lovers. The Greeks and Romans were skilled vintners, and they traded large earthenware jars filled with aromatic wine throughout the Mediterranean region. The Bible calls wine the "blood of the grape," and its use in the rituals of western religions continues to this day.

Wine is food. The alcoholic content of table wine is 14% or less; the body promptly converts this into energy. The fruit acids and salts contained in wine are beneficial, just as they are in the unfermented juice of fresh grapes. As an accompaniment to daily bread, wine is among life's temperate pleasures.

The ceremonious serving of wine at formal dinners and banquets has led many people to avoid offering wine in their homes or even ordering it in restaurants for fear of committing social blunders. They wonder what sort of wine goes with what food. Should it be red or white? Sweet or dry? What sort of glasses? Actually it is a mistaken notion that the serving of wine is governed by inflexible rules of etiquette. The only rigid rule is that people should drink the wine they like, when and how it suits them.

Generally speaking, there are certain affinities between wine and food. Just as bacon goes with eggs, so dry white wine goes well with fish. As fruit goes with cheese, so a "big" red wine goes well with steak. Not everybody agrees that such combinations are pleasing, but *most* people do. Familiarizing yourself with the wine and food combinations that most people prefer is an easy matter. (See page 221.) Once you have the traditional affinities in mind, serving or ordering wine becomes no more difficult than planning or ordering a meal.

KINDS OF WINE

There are many sorts of wine, but only four broad categories: *natural still wines,* such as claret or Sauternes, containing 14% alcohol or less; *sparkling,* such as Champagne, 14% or less; *fortified,* such as sherry, 16 to 23%; and *aromatized,* such as vermouth, 15-1/2 to 20%.

Wines are red, rosé (pink) or white. Nearly all red wines, including rosé, are dry or lacking in sugar. Port is a notable exception. White wines vary greatly in sweetness; some are very dry, some exceedingly sweet.

Domestic wines, especially those from the great wine-producing districts of California, are most readily available in this country. Imported wines come mainly from France, Germany and Italy, with much smaller quantities being shipped in from Switzerland, Chile and Greece. The finest domestic wines do not compare in quality with the finest French and German wines, but the wines produced here are *good* and getting better all the time. In purchasing wines, it's well to remember that a fine domestic wine is superior to an obscure imported wine offered as a "bargain." Foreign origin is no guarantee of excellence.

AMERICAN WINES

There are two main kinds: American or "native" wines and California wines. Native wines come from grape varieties peculiar to this country and grown mainly in New York and Ohio; they have distinctive flavors sometimes described as "grapey" or "wild." California wines are made from grape varieties originally imported from Europe and planted here. California wines generally resemble their European models.

Oddly enough, the person who sets out to buy a domestic

wine may find it more difficult to get exactly what he wants than if he were buying an imported wine. That is because the labeling of a domestic wine may not always correctly describe the contents. A label may read "Burgundy," but the wine may not taste anything like the Burgundy wine of France after which it was named. Some American vintners now label their wines by *grape varieties* rather than by European wine-type names, a practice that may seem complicated until you have acquired some knowledge of varietal names.

When you are buying a California dry white wine, grape names to watch for are: Riesling, Johannisberg Riesling, Pinot Blanc, Chardonnay, Sauvignon Blanc, Sylvaner, Traminer. Sweet white wine: sweet Semillon. Red wines: Cabernet, Pinot Noir, Gamay, Zinfandel, Petit Syrah, Mourestel, Barbera.

Probably you will not be able to buy native wines unless you live in the East. Watch for wine that originates in the Finger Lakes district in New York and Ohio's Lake Erie Islands. Among the best varietal names are Delaware, Elvira and Catawba.

Wine experiments being carried on at the University of California have led to notable improvements in domestic wine, and many conscientious vintners are striving to bring the quality of their products up to European standards. Among those making fine California wines are the Wente Brothers; Louis Martini; Louis Boist of Almaden Vineyards; the Marquis and Marquise de Pins and their president, Aldo Fabbrini; the Krug Brothers; and Inglenook Vineyards. In New York State, hybrid vines developed by Philip Wagner are now being planted, with the possibility of interesting changes in native wines.

Palatable domestic wines may be purchased for as little as a dollar; excellent wines, for around $1.60. When you are buying California, disregard vintage charts. The California climate, unlike that of France and Germany, is so even that the wines do not vary much from year to year.

FRENCH WINES

These are the greatest in the world. Their superb quality results from a fortuitous combination of soil, sunshine and centuries of experience in viticulture. Some French vineyards have been under cultivation since the Roman occupation. Generations of the same families have tilled the same soil.

The main sorts of French wines are identified by the names of the districts where the vineyards are located: *Bordeaux,* source of great clarets and famous sweet white wines; *Burgundy,* known for its rich, velvety red wines and for extraordinary dry white wines; *Rhône Valley,* famous for its sturdy reds and for pleasant rosé wines; *Alsace,* noted for refreshing light dry wines; *Loire Valley,* not so well known, but producing delightful white wines; and *Champagne,* producer of the world's most festive beverage.

Wine experts concede that Bordeaux is the finest of all wine-producing districts. It is a small area, about the size of Rhode Island, but the multitude of wines grown there is baffling to the novice, and can confuse even the experienced wine enthusiast. Shopping for Bordeaux wines in American cities is rather simple, however, because only a relatively small number reach here.

General familiarity with the wine types of the region is helpful in buying. Within Bordeaux are sub-districts, the names of which appear on labels: Médoc, Graves, Sauternes, and others. Most of the very famous clarets of Bordeaux originate in the Médoc; the very rich sweet white wines in Sauternes; sweet and a few somewhat dryish white wines in Graves. Knowing what part of Bordeaux a wine comes from therefore gives you a general idea of its character.

Many French wines are blends or mixtures of wines from several vineyards. These are the wines average Frenchmen drink every day. Some are good, but the best Bordeaux wines are "château-bottled." This phrase on a bottle means that the proprietor of the vineyard grew the grapes, did not blend the grapes or wine, and that he bottled and labeled the wine on his property. When the label is that of a renowned château, such as Château Margaux, the knowledgeable buyer knows he is getting his money's worth—provided the year the wine was produced was a "great" or "good" year. But what if the vintage year is not a good one? Then, perhaps, an inexpensive wine of the region may be just as good as a famous château bottling. (If you intend to familiarize yourself with the great wines of Bordeaux, or with any French wines, be sure to study Frank Schoonmaker's wine chart on pages 208–220.)

Some of the great names among Bordeaux red wines are: Château Haut-Brion, Château Lafite-Rothschild, Château Margaux, Château Latour, Château Ausone. Among whites: Château d'Yquem, Château Haut-Brion Blanc (this is dry), Château Olivier (dryish).

The château-bottling system is not followed in Burgundy. The wines of this region are made on small estates or tracts, often only an acre or so, and often operated by many joint owners. If the wines come from a famous vineyard, such as Romanée-Conti, the label will say so. Or the wine may bear the name of the parish if that is better known, or perhaps just the district name, if this is best known.

Genuine Burgundies are expensive and are widely imitated. They are "big" wines, full-bodied, with superb color and delicious bouquets. Some have velvety texture. Among great names of the red wines are Romanée-Conti (probably the finest of all red wines), Chambertin, Chambolle-Musigny, Pommard, Bonnes Mares, Échézeaux. Among the whites: Meursault, Montrachet, Aloxe-Corton, Chablis, Pouilly-Fuissé.

The best known of the Rhône Valley wines is Châteauneuf-du-Pape, a "big" wine that restaurateurs often wrongly list as a Burgundy. Another excellent Rhône wine is Côte-Rôtie. The dry Hermitage white wines are excellent, and from the lower part of the valley come the Tavel rosés, fine pink wines that are often hard to find in this country.

Alsatian wines, recognizable because of their distinctive long-necked bottles, vary from the light white Sylvaner and Riesling to the fuller Traminer and Gewürtztraminer. All are delightful drinking.

Among the Loire wines, Pouilly-Fumé is fresh, fruity and unusual. Muscadet is another pleasant wine from this area.

Champagne, symbol of gayety and good living, starts its fermentation in barrels like other wine, but then it is blended and bottled by skilled hands and receives a small amount of sugar syrup and yeast. It next goes through a second fermentation, forming carbonic acid gas within the bottle. Later in the process, all sediment is removed, and each bottle receives a "dosage" of sweetened aged wine. This dosage determines whether the Champagne shall be Brut (very dry), or, in ascending order of sweetness, Extra Dry, Dry, or Demi-Sec.

Good Champagne is never cheap, but it is no more costly than exceptionally fine bottles of Bordeaux or Burgundy. Some people, buying or serving wine on a festive occasion, make the mistake of believing that sparkling Burgundy is an adequate substitute for Champagne. As a matter of fact, sparkling Burgundy is a blend of inferior red wines, and it is always heavier than Champagne. It costs as much as a very good still wine. If cost is not important, serve Champagne; if cost must be considered, then serve a good natural wine.

Some of the great names in Champagne are Mumm, Piper Heidsieck, Moët et Chandon, Pol Roger, Pommery and Greno, Bollinger, Krug.

The price range of French wines is a good index of quality and scarcity. Good regional red Bordeaux: $1-$2; regional white Bordeaux: $1-$3; Château-bottled reds: $1.75-$9; Château-bottled whites: $1.25-$6.

Red Burgundies: $1.25-$9; white Burgundies: $1.25-$5; Rhône Valley, red and white: $1-$3; Rosé wines: $1-$3; Alsatian wines: $1.25-$2.75.

Champagne ranges from about $3.70 to $10.50, with around $6 buying an excellent bottle.

GERMAN WINES

White wines from the Rhine and Moselle districts of Germany are cherished by many wine lovers, and the supply in this country cannot always meet demand. In general, German wines tend to be more fruity and fragrant than French white wines. Some German wines are dryish, but the prevailing character of the wine is on the sweet side. Rhine wines tend to be full-bodied and long-lived, while the Moselles tend to be light and delicate, with marvelous bouquets. The Moselles should be drunk young.

Methods of grape harvesting in the Rhineland result in great variation in the flavor of wines. Only the ripest bunches are picked; the rest are left to ripen and be gathered later. Or only the ripest individual grapes are picked. The German vintner does not blend his wine, but makes it up in separate batches with "type names" indicating when and how the grapes were picked. Here is a translation of "type names."

A bottle of Rhine wine labeled *Auslese* means the wine was made from selected fully ripe bunches; *Spätlese* means the bunches were gathered late in the season; *Beerenauslese* means the bunches were picked at their very ripest point; *Trockenbeeren auslese* means the grapes were selected when they were semi-dried. Wines labeled "Auslese" and "Spätlese" tend to be dryish, while the other two labels indicate wine that is exceedingly rich and sweet.

On German wine labels, the name of the township that contains the vineyard usually precedes the vineyard's name. Some of the famous names to look for in buying Moselle wines are Berncasteler Doktor, Zeltinger Schlossberg, Piesporter Goldtröpfchen. Among Rhine wines: Schloss Johannisberg, Rüdesheimer Hauserweg, Rüdesheimer Schlossberg, Hocheimer Daubhaus.

The price range of German wines goes from around $1.75 to $15 or even more for "collector's items." Around $3 should buy a very good German wine.

ITALIAN WINES

Most Italian wine is consumed in Italy, and the purchaser here can find a fair selection only in cities like New York where the Italian population is large. In general, Italian red wines are rougher and earthier than their French counterparts, but several—if you can find them—have unusual fragrance and texture.

Chianti is the best-known Italian red wine, and when properly aged, is much softer than the wine that comes in the familiar straw-bound flasks. Look for mellowed Chianti in regular claret bottles. Barolo is a robust red wine with a violet bouquet. Barbera is similar but coarser.

White Chianti is sometimes available in this country. It is quite good. Other interesting Italian whites are dry Orvieto, Soave, Corvo, Capri, and Est, Est, Est.

Prices of Italian wines are reasonable: from around $1 to $2.50.

FORTIFIED WINES

The best Sherry comes from Spain, where for centuries the vintners near Jerez have made their wine by means of a unique blending method known as the *solera* system. Basically, this is a method of mixing older mellowed Sherry with newer wine. California Sherry, an imitation of the Spanish product, is not made by the *solera* system, although recently some California vintners have been experimenting with Spanish methods, with good results.

Sherry can be bone dry or very sweet. These words on the labels of Spanish Sherry tell you what you are getting: *Manzanilla,* extremely dry; *Fino,* also extremely dry; *Amontillado,* dryish and nutty; *Amoroso,* medium dry; *Oloroso,* sweet.

Port is made in the United States, Africa and South America, but the original and genuine Port comes only from the upper Douro River valley of northern Portugal. It is made and shipped under rigid legal delimitations, but these are not followed outside Portugal, with the consequence that California or South American "port" may be very good, but may not resemble the Portuguese product.

Grape brandy is the fortifying agent in Port, and the wine is always aged. The different sorts are: *Vintage Port,* which is wine of an exceptional year, aged in the bottle for perhaps as long as twenty years. It is a rough wine when young, then becomes mellow with a very fruity bouquet. English fathers sometimes buy Vintage Port at the birth of a son, and then father and son enjoy this mellowed wine when the boy reaches the age of twenty-one. *Crusted Port* is similar to *Vintage,* but not up to its elegant standard. Both *Vintage* and *Crusted Port* form heavy deposits in the bottle, and this makes shipping difficult without decanting into new bottles. *Ruby* and *Tawny Ports* are blended wines, matured in wood, with the deposit cleared away by fining. *Tawny* is relatively drier than *Ruby* and not so fruity as other Ports.

Ports from Portugal range from around $1.80 to $7.

Madeira, produced on a Portuguese island off the North African coast, was once as popular as Sherry is today. Many American fortunes in shipping were built on the Madeira trade, but around 1900 the fashion of drinking Madeira suddenly waned. Even so, there are quite a few people, especially women, who like it as a mid-afternoon drink, along with cookies or a biscuit.

The wine is made from ripe grapes, fortified with brandy made from the wine, and matured at high temperature in special hothouses. Most Madeira is sweet. The driest is Sercial, while Malmsey is very sweet. Prices are in about the same range as Port and Sherry.

AROMATIC WINES

The best-known aromatic wine is Vermouth—the dry French and the sweet Italian. The dry Vermouth is a blended and aged wine containing some 40 herbs, plants and flavoring agents. The sweet Vermouth is based on sweeter white wine infused with herbs and a little quinine. Domestic Vermouths are now about as good as the imported brands.

STORING WINE

In general, wines like a temperature between 55 and 60°. Five°, more or less, will not damage them. The main precaution is not to subject them to constant or abrupt changes in temperature. The storage problem is usually simple for restaurateurs and home owners who have cool cellars, but difficult for apartment dwellers who live in rooms kept at 70° or higher. Better not attempt to store large amounts of wine if the temperature is not right.

Store both natural and sparkling wines on their sides so that liquid keeps the cork wet. If the cork dries out, air seeps in and spoils natural oil; or gas escapes from Champagne, which then turns "flat." Fortified wines and liquors can sit upright. So can most California wines.

SERVING WINE

People enjoy wine because it looks good, smells good, tastes good. The ideal wineglass enhances this trio of sensations. The glass is clear; it is large enough so the wine can be swirled and "sniffed"; and it is a convenient shape for drinking. Through the years, certain wines have become associated with certain sorts of glasses, but present-day usage encourages the "all-purpose" glass: tulip-shaped, with a capacity of about 8 ounces. Such glasses are available nearly everywhere. In pouring wine, fill the glass only 1/3 to 1/2 full.

Serve the following wines chilled: all white wines; Champagne and other sparkling wines; rosé wines; dry Sherries and Madeiras. Do not chill until the wine is icy cold for this kills its flavor. About 45 to 50° is right. You can bring the wine to this temperature by refrigerating it for an hour or so, or by chilling it in a wine cooler 15 to 20 minutes.

Serve the following at room temperature: all red wines, except Beaujolais, which, if you wish, can be chilled slightly; Port, and the sweeter Madeiras and Sherries. Red wine should be opened about an hour before serving and permitted to "breathe"—this improves its bouquet.

Wine baskets are an affectation. They were invented to help servants move great Burgundies from the cellar without stirring up the sediment. If you have sedimented wines, decant them about an hour before serving. Or simply handle the bottle carefully. White wines seldom contain sediment, and to decant a white wine or to carry it in a basket is silly.

VINTAGE CHART FOR 1950–1960

By Frank Schoonmaker

Membre Diplômé de l'Académie du Vin de France

Of the many diverse pleasures that wine-drinking affords, one of the most singular is the extent to which it permits us, quite literally and actually, to recapture and relive the past. For what we are tasting when we open a fine old bottle is simply the warmth of one particular, memorable summer, the fragrance of one special autumn, unlike all others.

This is one of the reasons that a wine that carries a vintage is basically more interesting than one that does not, even if it is no better or less good, as is occasionally the case. There is something agreeable, even if a little nostalgic, about being able to say, to one's friends, "This is the wine they made the summer we were in Paris," or "Tonight we will drink the wine they made the year our son was born."

For reasons such as these, and others less valid and more commercial, vintage charts have become very much the vogue—one of the indispensable accessories of the well-dressed man, like cuff links and a collection of credit cards. This is perhaps to be deplored, for the best of such vintage charts is really nothing more than a sort of signpost or reminder: it cannot possibly be a guide. No one could review a book or a play, or even comment adequately on a well-cooked dish or a flower show or a football game, in terms of one or two digits or stars or a couple of words. How then present in capsule form the vastly varied wines of a thousand different vineyards?

Then, too, a good many of these vintage vade mecums are put out by merchants who have large stocks of certain vintages they wish to sell, and therefore tend, despite themselves, to favor; others are prepared by people who have never tasted one-tenth, let alone one-half, of the wines they presume to rate.

What follows, attempts at least to be something a little different—a pretty detailed description of the wines of each major district and each year. It is based on carefully kept notes, made at the time of tasting, covering some four thousand wines comparatively tasted every year (except for the war years) since 1935, plus a good many *dégustations* made as an amateur (in both the French and the English senses) during the preceding decade. The comments are as disinterested and honest as I can make them, and although they are based inevitably on personal opinion, this is at least an informed opinion, and I have no ax to grind.

Ratings, 1 to 20, are based on the relative value and quality of the wines today, *not on what they were when originally produced or first marketed. 18-20=Very Great. 16-17=Great. 15=Very Good. 14=Good. 12-13=Fair. 11=Poor. 10 and under=Very Poor. In most cases, for 1960, it is too early to judge, and the evaluations are wholly tentative. Where no ratings are given, the wines are either too old to be interesting or no longer on the market in 1961.*

BORDEAUX

1960. What the French call a "jealous" year, with wide variations in quality from one township, and indeed from one vineyard, to the next. Overpublicized during the early summer of '60 when the outlook was rosy, it is turning out to be far from a great vintage—better, to be sure, than '56, '54, and '51 (which is faint praise), less good than '50 . . . perhaps, if we are lucky, on a par with 1958 . . . about 14/20. This for the reds; the drier whites are considerably more successful, 16/20, but the Sauternes and sweeter whites were touched by mold and deserve no more than 11/20.

1959. Extremely great, possibly the best since World War II, especially in the Médoc, where the red wines promise to surpass even the wonderful 1953's; less remarkable in St. Emilion and Pomerol. Already overpriced, they will become practically unprocurable as soon as they are bottled and shipped, in 1962, and those who get them will have treasures, indeed. Soon ready but superbly balanced, they should have a long and glorious life. The whites are no less outstanding, and an 18/20 grade for both is perhaps too low.

1958. Generally underrated, a good and useful year, especially in red wines. These will be sooner ready than the '57's, in many cases quite as good, and far less expensive: for the next few years they will be the best values on the market in the way of château-bottled Claret, deserve 14/20. The whites, very much on the dry side, are less pleasing, rate 12/20 to 14/20.

1957. Proclaimed with great trumpeting (which now seems to be the fashion in the Bordelais) as "a very great vintage," '57 is actually nothing of the kind, but a year of hard, often harsh, deep-colored wines, high in tannin and acid, recalling the '48's, 37's, and '26's. Conceivably, a few of the best château wines may, ten years from now, prove magnificent, but this is far from certain and indeed unlikely. 15/20. The whites are less good, 13/20.

1956. Small wines, a few of them agreeable in their modest way. 11/20.

1955. A great year, and one that has surprised and delighted almost everybody. Considered "good," or possibly "very good," with some hesitation, at the start, it nows deserves a higher grade, in the Médoc, than '52, and is better than '53 in St. Emilion and Pomerol. The '55's are now the best Clarets generally available, but they are even now becoming scarce—within a matter of months they will be hard to find, and a great deal more expensive. 17/20. The dry whites, never remarkable, are growing old; the sweeter whites were only fair to begin with. 13/20 or 14/20.

1954. There were a few light, fairly pleasing red wines; most of them are now on the decline. With malice toward none, let's say 11/20.

1953. An extremely great year, one graced (like '59 and indeed '29) with extraordinary softness, elegance, fragrance, and fruit almost from the very beginning. It would be unfair to expect such charms to last indefinitely, and only the very best Médocs are likely to improve much further. Most of the others, including *all* the St. Emilions and Pomerols, can advisedly be drunk in the next three to five years. For the moment, perhaps 18/20—which is too low for the best and too high for the others. The white Graves are now growing old, and so are all the other white wines except the Sauternes—these (only the sweet ones) deserve 16/20.

1952. In St. Emilion and Pomerol, the best vintage (excepting 1947) since World War II, and perhaps even since 1928. The Médocs are sturdy but much less attractive, may outlast the '53's but will never be as good. 15/20 to 18/20, but note, however, that the lesser wines are gone. The very best whites deserve perhaps 14/20—forget the others.

1951. Long since gone and no loss either.

1950. Very good. Fine, rather light wines, which developed well and received less appreciation than they deserved . . . and still deserve, for that matter, when you can find them. 14/20 for the Clarets; the whites are over the hill, 11/20 or less.

Unlike the Burgundies, the great château Clarets of the first great postwar years (1945, 1947, 1949) are now at their absolute peak of quality, and some of us who drank them promptly have lived to regret our impatience. They are practically unprocurable today, and acquiring them is less a matter of money than of good fortune.

BURGUNDY

1960. The spring and early summer of 1960 promised great things—then came the rains. The net result is disappointing: in red wines, a huge crop but, with rare exceptions, wines deficient in color, character, and body. 12/20. The whites are vastly better, fresh, light, attractive but probably short lived. 15/20.

1959. A truly incomparable year, which has been and can fairly be called the "Vintage of the Century." In quantity, almost double the average; in quality, unsurpassed since 1900. The red wines are maturing quickly, and there is little chance of their being long-lived. On the other hand, it is hard to imagine how they could be better than they are and will be for the next five years—silky, *bouqueté,* beautifully balanced, full of grace and distinction and charm. In red wines, 20/20. The whites are very different—rich, full-bodied, almost overpowering, possibly a little lacking in breed; also probably short-lived, but 18/20.

1958. Spotty and hardly more than passable in red wines, deserves about 12/20. The whites are another matter: fragrant, light, and fine, they recall the splendid 1950's, and many experts rate them ahead of the 1959's. 18/20.

1957. Big, sturdy, firm red wines, maturing slowly and almost certain to outlast the 1959's, although presently less attractive. Now about 16/20 and bound to improve. The whites less good; only the very best of them ever lost their early greenness, or will. 14/20 on the average.

1956. Poor and best forgotten. A few passable whites.

1955. A great year. Red wines which have surpassed all expectations are now, on the whole, the best red Burgundies for present drinking, or until the '59's come along. In many cases their development was arrested and their character somewhat affected, in cellar, by the intensely cold winter of 1955-56. They have outlived this handicap and, while rarely sensational, are consistently fine. 16/20. The whites, also good, were rather light and are no longer improving—14/20.

1954. Poor with almost no exceptions.

1953. An extremely great year, not far behind 1959 in quality. The reds were charmers from the beginning but, less well-balanced than the '59's, never gave promise of long life, and many of them have begun to throw sediment and give other evidences of senescence. Originally 19/20, they are down to 15/20 today, but there are a few magnificent exceptions. Drink them. The whites were never as good as the reds, and never as good as the '52's. They will gain nothing by further keeping.

1952. Sturdy red wines, a little lacking in grace and fruit, which are beginning to overtake the more attractive '53's; they are good, not great—14/20. The whites were the best of the past two decades, but they, too, alas, will soon be gone. 15/20.

1951. *Requiescat in pace.*

1950. The reds, never much good, are gone. 11/20. The whites, on the other hand, were underrated and truly remarkable. Few can still be found, but a surprising percentage of these, if properly stored, are extremely fine. Now 14/20.

NOTE: In the way of older vintages, there is precious little that can be recommended: the very best 1947's of the Côte de Beaune are still magnificent, and from the Côte de Nuits one finds occasional bottles of 1949, 1947, and even 1945 that have withstood the passing years. The rest is history.

BEAUJOLAIS

Engaging, fruity, fresh, eminently drinkable, Beaujolais is a wine that improves hardly at all with age. In Paris, as in Lyon, it is consumed (as "open wine") cheerfully and copiously as soon as it reaches the precocious age of three months, and a Beaujolais three years old is considered past its prime. We in America must perforce be a little more patient and wait at least until the wine is bottled and can stand shipment, which takes from nine months to a year. But here, too, we can almost say "the younger, the better," though with a few reservations, since a Beaujolais of a poor year, however delicious in a French *bistro,* rarely travels well.

1960. An enormous crop, one of the largest in history, but mostly just *vins de comptoir,* light wines that will be served by the glass and never bottled. A few, carefully selected, will be at least fair and some of them even good. 12/20.

1959. A great year, though less remarkable than in Burgundy proper. There were a few failures, but most of the wines are firm, sound, of truly excellent quality—they are ready now, but the good ones will certainly hold for another two or three years. 17/20.

1958. Rather attractive at first, these have grievously disappointed us, and they are finished. 12/20.

1957. Sturdy, very full-bodied, perhaps lacking in fruit and that velvety quality which the French call *gras,* but long-lived. 16/20.

Of earlier years, a few of the very best '55's are still sound. The others need not concern us.

CÔTES DU RHÔNE

1960. The Rhone Valley wines do not follow, on the whole, the same vintage pattern as the rest of France, and 1960, at least in Tavel and Châteauneuf-du-Pape, was a better year than 1959. The excellent rosés will be in bottle and ready to drink by September, and the reds are decidedly promising. 16/20.

1959. Of all the fine wine districts in Western Europe, only the province of Piedmont, in Italy, and the Rhone Valley, in France, failed to produce something outstanding in '59. Fairly good, 14/20, no more.

1958. Just passable. The red wines, much lighter than usual, are agreeable, fruity, now ready; the rosés are already showing signs of age. 12/20.

1957. A great year. Very small crop, high quality; big, full-bodied wines that are developing slowly and will be long-lived. 16/20 except for the rosés, which are already past their prime.

1956. Mediocre. 10/20.

1955. Very great. The Châteauneuf-du-Pape now at its

superb peak; the Hermitage developing magnificently. 18/20. NOTE: Authentic Rhone wines older than the 1955's are extremely rare, and bottles labeled "1949," "1947," "1945," etc., should be regarded with skepticism, especially if the wine has not thrown a heavy sediment. When you can find them, the genuine 1952's are extraordinary, deserve 18/20 or even possibly 19/20.

LOIRE VALLEY

1960. Considerably better than in the rest of France. Quite satisfactory wines, especially in the Muscadet country, Anjou, and Saumur. Perhaps 14/20 on the average.
1959. A bounteous and wonderful vintage. Practically all the Loire hillsides, from Pouilly-Fumé and Sancerre down to Muscadet, shared in this good fortune, and produced fruity full-bodied wines; some of the whites and rosés are showing signs of age. 15/20 to 19/20.
1958. Somewhat uneven. Wines rather dry and light, but many of them very pleasant. 13/20.
NOTE: A few older Loire wines are still of more than passing interest when they can be found, notably the 1953's, which were magnificent everywhere, the 1955 and 1957 red wines of Chinon and St. Nicholas-de-Bourgeuil, the dry but fragrant 1955 Vouvrays.

ALSACE

1960. Fair. Very large crop, wines rather on the light side. 13/20.
1959. An extremely great year, as in Germany. The Rieslings were particularly successful, racy, fruity, among the best since World War II. 19/20. The Gewürztraminers, as is often the case in warm, dry years, are a bit low in acid and have to be selected with great care. 16/20.

1958. A good year; wines fresh, light, and attractive, on the dry side. 15/20.

1957. The bigger wines, most particularly the Gewürztraminers, have developed beyond all expectations, and some of them can only be described as superb. The smaller wines, however, are hard and mediocre. To strike an average, perhaps 16/20.

NOTE: 1955, 1953, and 1952 were all three good years, but Alsatian wines never gain much by keeping, and, frankly, the younger wines are much better today.

CHAMPAGNE

A detailed vintage chart for Champagne cannot help being a little ridiculous: in five years out of ten the wine never even pretends to go to the consumer in an unblended state, and admittedly would be less good if it did; and what proportion of which vintage goes into a nonvintage Champagne is a well-kept trade secret, and not for us common people, whose only real function anyway is to drink Champagne and pay for it.

It is certainly more sensible, therefore, to reserve comment on what might be called the "buried" years—those that have disappeared into the nonvintage—and discuss only those that have been, or may be, presented as *millésimes:* 1960 (?), 1959, 1958 (?), 1957, 1955, 1953, 1952, and 1950. We may as well forget 1950, too, which came along when the '49's and '47's were still famous and unsold, and which appeared only on a few rare but very good bottles from producer-growers.

1960. Will probably not carry a vintage. Passably good, light wines, most of them destined to be blended with the heavier '59's, which they will complement nicely. Alone, no better than 13/20.

1959. Will unquestionably be shipped as a vintage although, in this case, as the French say, *"la mariée était trop belle"*—it was *too* good a year. The grapes ripened superbly and the quantity was satisfactory, but the wines were extremely full-bodied, too high in alcohol, and they proved hard to re-ferment into sparkling wine. Doubtless there will be some superb *cuvées,* but others unquestionably will prove very heavy, lacking in sprightliness, delicacy, and charm. 15/20.

1958. Uneven, but fairly good. Some houses may ship it as a vintage but they will probably be in the minority. At least 13/20, possibly deserves more.

1957. Almost certainly will emerge as a vintage although the crop was pitifully small and the wines, so far, seem green and rather hard. Not a great year. 14/20.

1955. Extremely good, better than expected, soon to make their bow. Sound, well-balanced wines, with a good deal of finesse, more attractive in many cases than the '53's. 16/20.

1953. Highly touted and extravagantly praised, especially at the beginning, the '53's are now obviously far below the '52's in quality: very full wines, high in alcohol, they now lack distinction and grace, and these are qualities which Champagnes rarely acquire as they grow older. To be drunk, not laid away. A big year, but not an especially attractive wine. 16/20.

1952. A very great year, certainly the best of the past two decades, quite comparable to that "incomparable" year, 1928. The wines seem to have everything—great class, bouquet, a nice equilibrium of lightness and body, a charm that makes them immediately engaging, and other qualities which would seem to assure them long life. 19/20 as a minimum.

RHINE AND MOSELLE

1960. Somewhat uneven, poor in the Moselle, fair in the Rheingau, very good in the Pfalz. A large crop, rather light wines, should be comparatively inexpensive and good values. 11/20 to 15/20.

1959. An exceedingly great year, certainly unsurpassed since the last war and in many ways comparable to 1921. But wine-making methods in Germany have changed greatly in the last four decades; the wines are now bottled much earlier than they were, in order to conserve their freshness and fruit. As a result, the 1959's will prove shorter lived, but most of them, on the other hand, are now ready to drink, and all of them will be before 1961 is out. Their average quality is amazingly high (though some of the commoner and cheaper ones are flat and dull, being too low in acid); the estate bottlings, from the driest to the sweetest, have great ripeness and fruit—they are as full-bodied as the '49's and '53's, but with more distinction. As always, there are some variations in quality from one district or township to another: the '59 Saar wines (Ockfeners, Wiltingers, Scharzhofbergers) are magnificent, as are those of the Ruwer, and on the Moselle, Piesport, Berncastel, and Graach surpassed themselves. Most of the Rheingau wines, too, are extraordinary, especially those of Schloss Vollrads, Rauenthal, and Johannisberg. Remarkable *Beeren-* and *Trockenbeerenauslesen* were produced, notably in the Pfalz. Truly, on the whole, a "Vintage of the Century." 20/20.

1958. An excellent year. Light and charming wines, dry, fresh, and flowery, perhaps even more agreeable, for everyday use, than the more imposing and formidable '59's. Not too expensive, they are excellent values, and deserve 16/20.

1957. An uneven year. A few good wines, but many that are hard, lacking in fruit, and unattractive. 12/20.

1956. Extremely poor.

1955. A very great year, but all save a few of the biggest wines are light, delicate, and astonishingly low in alcohol, often under nine per cent. They make up in fragrance what they lack in authority. Now 14/20.

1954. One of the worst on record.

1953. A very great year, but all save a few of the biggest wines—the *Auslesen,* etc.—are now past their prime. Rate between 14/20 and 18/20 today.

1952. A very good year, but on the whole now too old. Perhaps 13/20 today.

1951. Generally poor. Now off the market.
1950. A good year. Light, pleasant wines. Most of them now too old. Rhines worth only 11/20, Moselles less.

ITALY

In the past ten or fifteen years, Italian wines have made thousands of new friends in the United States. Most of us like Italian food, and nothing is better with it than Italian wine; many of us have visited Italy, and found the local wines both excellent and interesting—uncomplicated, appetizing, and attractive.

The majority of Italian wines are made to be drunk when young—only a few reds (the finer Chiantis, certain rare Valpolicellas, and the Barolos and Barbarescos of the Province of Piedmont) improve materially with age.

Almost all of the white wines, and the few rosés which are exported (Chiarello, Chiaretto, etc.) are at their best when under three years old, and for these a vintage chart is quite unnecessary.

The finest grades of Chianti are shipped in ordinary wine bottles, like Bordeaux, and these *do* improve with aging. The others in the familiar straw-covered *fiaschi* are ready to drink well before their third birthday, and in most of the restaurants of Florence you will find them served even younger.

For those worth laying down here are the best years:
Chianti—1955, 1957, 1958.
Valpolicella—1955, 1958, 1959.
Barolo, Barbaresco—1952, 1955, 1956, 1957.

NEW YORK STATE

The variations from one year to another are much greater in the Finger Lakes district than in California, and, for some odd reason, vintages that are outstanding in France and Germany, tend to be good in New York State as well. Thus, in the past decade or so, 1949, 1953, 1955, 1957, and 1959 have all been above average, and 1960, also, far from bad. Not all New York State wines by any means, however, carry a vintage; most of them are better when they are young.

CALIFORNIA

The fine wine-producing district of California, north and east and south of San Francisco Bay, is blessed with an extremely equable climate and is admirably suited to the growing of superior wine grapes.

However, here, as in the Rhone Valley of France, and as in northern Spain and Italy, there are not those wide differences between one year and another which are alternately the delight and the despair of most European vintners.

California, it has been said, with some justification, "has no bad years," but of course (and this follows logically enough), no great or extraordinary years, either; a vintage on a bottle of California wine is really not an indication of quality but a statement of age. In many cases, and on many of the best wines, the vintage is omitted altogether.

California's white wines and excellent rosés should all be drunk young and are generally sent to market when they are ready to drink. The best reds (Pinot Noir and Cabernet Sauvignon) are aged in wood before bottling and quite often in bottle before they leave the winery. The good ones will all improve further if laid away, but no expert could hope to distinguish between, for example, the 1957's, the 1958's, and the 1959's with any degree of consistency.

TRADITIONAL AFFINITIES BETWEEN FOOD AND WINE

These are suggestions, not rules. Most people like the combinations listed, but your personal preference should make the decision. Restaurateurs and people who entertain large groups find it best to adhere to the traditional affinities rather than to experiment. They can be sure that time-tested combinations of food and wine will please nearly everybody.

Champagne is congenial with food throughout meals. As an appetizer, serve *Brut;* serve *Brut* or *Extra Dry* up to dessert; serve the sweeter Champagnes only as dessert wines.

FOOD	DOMESTIC WINE	IMPORTED WINE
Appetizers, snacks, hors d'oeuvres	Dry Sherry, Rosé Wines	Dry Sherry, Dry Madeira Rosé Wines Chablis Muscadet Dry Rhines and Moselles Dry Italian Whites Italian Vermouth, iced
Oysters on the half shell		Chablis
Soup	Medium Sherry	Medium Sherry Madeira (not too sweet)
Shellfish, fish dishes, cold chicken and turkey.	Dry Semillon Johannisberg Riesling Riesling Pinot Blanc Chardonnay Sauvignon Blanc Folle Blanche Sylvaner Traminer Native Whites	Chablis and other white Burgundies: Meursault Montrachet Pouilly-Fuissé Muscadet Dryish Grâves Dry Rhines and Moselles White Chianti and other Dry Italian Whites Alsatian Wines
Salmon	Dry Whites, as above Rosé Wines	Dry Whites, as above Rosé Wines Beaujolais

FOOD	DOMESTIC WINE	IMPORTED WINE
Roasts and chops (except pork and veal), pot roasts, liver	Cabernet, Zinfandel and other Light Reds Barbera	Red Bordeaux Red Burgundy
Veal roasts and chops	Dry Whites	Dry Whites
Pork roasts and chops	Dry Whites Rosé Wines	Dry Whites Rosé Wines Champagne
Roast ham	Beer Rosé Wines	Beer Rosé Wines
Full-flavored red meats, all game, including venison and duck	Pinot Noir Gamay Burgundy	Red Burgundies Red Rhône Wines Red Chianti Barolo Barbera
Salad bowls	Riesling and other light Dry Whites	Alsatian Dry Rhines and Moselles
Nuts, cheese	All the robust Reds suggested for meat and game Port Sweeter Sherries	All the robust Reds suggested for meat and game Port Sweeter Sherries
Desserts	Sweet Semillon California Sauterne	Sweet Rhine Wines Sauternes
Coffee	Brandies and Liqueurs Sweeter Sherries Port	Cognac and Liqueurs Sweeter Sherries Madeira Port

DISPENSING DRAUGHT BEER †

There is probably no beverage as sensitive to mishandling as draught beer. Yet three simple fundamental principles control the many details involved in the proper dispensing of perfect "brewery fresh" draught beer. These are *proper refrigeration, cleanliness* and *proper pressures.*

Since draught beer is perishable, it must not be exposed to warm temperatures. The retailer must preserve it by providing equipment that will maintain the temperature of the beer in the barrel bewteen 38°–42° F. These temperatures should be maintained throughout the dispensing equipment so that the beer in the glass as it is served to the consumer will be at 38°–42° F. This range of temperature seems to satisfy the majority of tastes and is too small a variation to affect its flavor or quality.

Cleanliness is a most vital consideration. The beer faucets, tubing, hose, coils, taps, and vents, including direct draw systems, must be thoroughly cleaned at regular intervals. Glasses must be immaculate and sparklingly clean. No effort should be spared to keep the bar clean and bright. Odors and appearances that might be disagreeable must be avoided.

Proper pressure in the barrel is very important. To maintain "brewery fresh" taste in the beer, its natural or normal carbonation must be preserved. The dispensing equipment through which the beer flows must have a pressure that corresponds to the normal carbonation of the beer at the temperature of the beer in the barrel. The size and length of the coil in the dispensing equipment will determine the pressure to be used.

With the dispensing equipment properly set up, the retailer

† Prepared by Anheuser-Busch, Inc.

is ready to serve draught beer. To draw beer, hold the glass at an angle close to the lip of the faucet—open the faucet all the way—lower and straighten up the glass as the beer flows into it so that the desired foam is formed—about one-half inch before the glass is full close the faucet all the way. The foam will rise to the top of the glass, completely filling it without overflowing. A desirable glass of draught beer should include about 20% foam.

BEERS

Half and Half (American Style)

Fill glass half full of Beer and fill up with Porter.

Half and Half ('Alf and 'Alf) (English Style)

Fill glass half full of Beer and fill up with Ale.

FOOD TO GO WITH DRINKS

The problem of what food to serve with drinks is easy to solve these days. The markets offer an abundance of wonderful delicacies. There are so many appetizing things that can be made up easily for a cocktail party that no one should ever have to resort to the old potato chip and salted peanut routine. Nor should anyone feel compelled to offer the dits and doots popular a few years ago. Trays of tired sections of bread with colored cream cheese and odd designs are actually not very appealing to most people. Besides, such dits and doots require far too much preparation. My advice is to take it easy. Serve simple, substantial appetizers.

Here are a few of the simplest things to serve with drinks. Most of them can be held in reserve on the shelf or in the refrigerator. Nearly all can be readied quickly when friends and neighbors drop by for drinks.

NUTS

You may buy salted nuts of all kinds in tins. They keep fresh for a long time. The peanut, of course, is the standby, but other varieties are even better and more original as accompaniments to drinks.

Try *Macadamia nuts* from Hawaii with a taste rather like a hot biscuit; *fava beans,* roasted (not really a nut but in the same category); *chick peas,* toasted and salted—very crisp and with a most distinctive flavor; *pistachio nuts*—the large white, salted ones are the best; *walnuts*—these delectable nuts, toasted and salted, are too often neglected; *Mexican sunflower seeds*—crisp and well salted; *giant pecans,* toasted and well salted.

It is no trick to salt your own almonds and filberts and the difference in price is astonishing. Oregon filberts, in particular, are unusual and tasty cocktail bits if treated correctly.

Here are a few ideas for preparing nuts that can be eaten warm or stored in glass jars.

SALTED ALMONDS IN THEIR COATS

Spread 1 pound of shelled almonds in their skins in a large, flat baking pan or cookie sheet. Sprinkle with salt to taste and dot lightly with butter. Bake at 350° for 25–35 minutes, or until the nuts are nicely toasted but not charred in flavor. Taste often after the first 25 minutes and be on the alert for the prize moment. Remove the nuts, and let them cool on absorbent paper.

VARIATIONS

Blanched Almonds: Place the nuts in boiling water for 2–3 minutes to loosen the skins. Slip the skins off with the fingers. Place the blanched almonds in a baking pan or sheet and add 4 tablespoons butter or 1/3 cup oil. Toast in the oven at 350° until nicely browned and crisp. Sprinkle with salt to taste and drain on absorbent paper.

Garlic Almonds: Proceed as in either of the recipes above but add Spice Islands garlic seasoning powder to the nuts before putting them in the oven. Or blend 2 cloves of finely chopped fresh garlic with 1/3 cup oil and pour over the nuts before roasting. Salt to taste when you remove the nuts from the oven.

Curried Almonds: Add 1 tablespoon curry powder to the mixture above and swirl the nuts around in it as they roast.

Chili Almonds: Substitute good chili powder for curry and mix well with the nuts.

SALTED FILBERTS

Place filberts in flat baking pan with salt and butter or oil. Toast at 350° for 25–35 minutes. Drain on absorbent paper.

Garlic or Curry Filberts: Place 1 pound pecan halves in a

flat baking pan. Dot with butter and sprinkle with salt. Bake at 350° for 20 minutes or until the nuts are toasted and crisp. Drain on absorbent paper.

Garlic or Curry or Chili Pecans: Add seasonings as above.

SALTED PEANUTS

Proceed as with salted pecans.

DUNKS AND DIPS

The dunk is practically an indoor sport. A bowl of one or two different mixtures with raw vegetables, potato chips or tiny codfish balls enhances almost any sort of gathering. Dunks are made with a mayonnaise or sour cream base, and some have cream cheese or cottage cheese added for body.

HERB DUNK FOR RAW VEGETABLES

Combine 1-1/2 pints of sour cream with 1 teaspoon salt or more; 1 cup chopped spinach; 1/2 cup each chopped parsley, chives and dill and 1 clove garlic, chopped fine. Blend thoroughly and let chill for 2 hours before serving.

VARIATIONS

Mustard: Omit the dill and add 2 tablespoons French mustard and 1 teaspoon dry mustard to the mixture.

Pungent: Omit dill and add 1/4 cup chopped green pepper, 1/2 cup chopped cucumber and 1 tablespoon chili powder and 1 teaspoon freshly ground black pepper.

Anchovy: Add 1 can anchovy fillets, chopped fine, a hard-boiled egg, chopped fine, and 1 teaspoon orégano. Omit the dill. Add 3 tablespoons capers.

Tart: Add 1/4 cup chopped pickled onions and 4 tablespoons capers to the basic mix, omitting the dill. Add 3 tablespoons lemon juice and some freshly ground black pepper.

VEGETABLES FOR DUNKING

Any raw vegetable, crisp and cold, goes with these sauces. Some of the less usual ones are tiny *raw asparagus tips* (once tasted they make you wonder why you have eaten only cooked asparagus all these years); the *finger* or *seedless avocado,* now becoming more popular and plentiful; *Chinese water chestnuts,* speared with a toothpick, excellent because of their delightful crispness.

The regulars are *carrots, green onions, cauliflower flowerets, turnips, radishes* (including the *Japanese radish* cut in slices), *zucchini, cucumber fingers, cherry* or *plum tomatoes, celery, anise, fennel,* and *endive stalks.* All very pleasant to munch with cocktails.

DIPS FOR SHRIMP AND OTHER SHELLFISH OR CHICKEN OR TURKEY FINGERS

These are suitable for vegetables but are primarily for sea food.

SHRIMP DIP

Combine 2 cups mayonnaise with 1/2 cup chili sauce, 1 tablespoon anchovy paste, 1/2 cup chopped green onions, 2 hard-boiled eggs, chopped rather fine, 1/4 cup parsley, chopped fine, salt and pepper to taste.

PLAIN DIP

It's hard to surpass a fine mayonnaise made from good olive oil, egg yolks, salt, pepper, mustard and lemon juice. Perfect with shrimp or lobster or with any fish on toothpicks.

ORIENTAL DIP

Combine 1 cup mayonnaise, 1 cup sour cream, 2 tablespoons chopped ginger, 1 tablespoon soy sauce, 2 tablespoons chopped water chestnuts, 2 cloves of garlic, chopped fine, 1/2 cup chopped green onions, 1 tablespoon chopped Chinese parsley (cilantro or fresh coriander) if available, 1/4 cup chopped parsley. This is elegant with either shrimp or lobster.

SPREADS

This is another easy approach to entertaining. Arrange a big bowl of spread surrounded by thinly sliced and buttered (or not buttered, as you will) rye bread, pumpernickel, lavash in pieces, cracker bread, fine protein bread–any selection of good breads and crackers.

LIEDERKRANZ SPREAD

Liederkranz cheeses should be selected carefully. They should be soft but not runny and have a good ripe flavor. Mash them with a fork, adding 2 tablespoons chopped chives, 1/4 cup chopped parsley, 3 tablespoons capers, 1 teaspoon dry mustard, 1 tablespoon Worcestershire sauce and about 1/4 cup sour cream. Beat well, taste for seasoning and let the mixture ripen for an hour or two before serving. Sprinkle with paprika and chopped parsley before serving. If the spread seems thin, fold in a little cream cheese to give it body.

CRABMEAT SPREAD

Combine 1 pound or 2 cans crabmeat with 1 seeded and shredded cucumber, 1/4 cup chopped parsley, 1/4 cup chopped green onions and 1/2 cup mayonnaise. Season with lemon juice and 1/4 cup of rum. Let stand for 2 hours and drain. Arrange in a bowl and sprinkle with chopped parsley.

AVOCADO SPREAD or POOR MAN'S BUTTER

Mash 3 very ripe avocados and add 1/2 cup chopped green onions, 1 teaspoon salt, 1 teaspoon chili powder and 2 tablespoons chili sauce. Blend well by hand or in the electric mixer. Sprinkle lavishly with chopped parsley. Good as a spread with toasted tortillas or with carnitas.

RAW MEAT SPREAD

This is an all-time favorite with drinks. Combine 1-1/2 pounds ground round steak with no fat (have it freshly ground), 1 egg, 1 teaspoon dry mustard, 1 tablespoon French mustard, 2 tablespoons A-1 sauce, 1/2 cup chopped green onions, 1 clove garlic, cut fine. Blend well and place in a large bowl and sprinkle with chopped green onions and parsley. Serve with generous amounts of pumpernickel and hot toast.

ROQUEFORT CHEESE SPREAD

Combine 1 pound Roquefort cheese with 1/2 pound cream cheese, 1/4 pound butter, 1 teaspoon freshly ground black pepper, 1 teaspoon dry mustard, 3 tablespoons Worcestershire sauce and 1/4 cup Cognac. Beat well until the mixture is well blended. Refrigerate in small jars. This is an excellent cheese course at dinner.

LANGLOIS BLUE VEIN CHEESE SPREAD

Langlois cheese is one of the great achievements of American cheesemaking. Here is a recipe from Mrs. Hansen, head of the Langlois firm:

Combine 1 pound Langlois blue with an equal quantity of cream cheese and 1-1/2 cups chopped walnuts. Moisten with a little Cognac. Cream it well and store in small jars.

HELEN BROWN'S IN-A-MINUTE CHEESE SPREAD

This is based on a cheese mixture called Whiz, which is to be found almost everywhere. Combine it with A-1 sauce,

Worcestershire, mustard, chili powder or sauce, or with chopped green onions and salt and pepper. Serve with crackers or pumpernickel. Easy, good and very quick.

CHEESE BALLS

Combine 1 pound cream cheese with 1 pound cottage cheese, 2 tablespoons each chopped green onions and parsley and 1 cup chopped nuts. Season with salt and pepper and dry mustard. Form into small balls, roll in chopped parsley or chopped nuts, and chill for a half hour or so. Serve impaled on toothpicks.

HOT PARMESAN DELIGHTS

This recipe was perfected by the food consultant to the Taylor Wine Company, in Hammondsport, New York. It is simple and tasty.

Combine 1 cup mayonnaise, 1/2 cup grated Parmesan cheese, 2 teaspoons Worcestershire sauce, dash of onion seasoning or 1 tablespoon chopped green onions. Add 1-1/2 tablespoons Sherry or Cognac and blend well. Spread on toast squares or on crackers, and sprinkle with a little additional cheese. Brown under the broiler and serve very hot.

PÂTÉS TO BE USED WITH COCKTAILS

HOME-STYLE PÂTÉ

This can be used for cocktail snacks or for sandwiches.

Purchase 1-1/2 pounds lamb's liver, in thin slices, or pork liver; also 1-1/2 pounds ground pork and 1 pound salt pork, cut in thin slices. A good addition is a pound of pork loin cut in paper-thin sices.

Hard boil 4 eggs. Then poach the liver in a skillet with 1

cup wine—red wine or Sherry—1 bay leaf, 1 teaspoon salt, 2 teaspoons freshly ground black pepper, 2 cloves garlic. Let it cook slowly, and if there is not enough wine to cover add a little consommé or stock. When the liver is very soft pull it apart and chop it rather coarse. Combine with the ground pork, 1 teaspoon thyme, 3 garlic cloves, chopped fine, 1 teaspoon dry mustard, 1/2 cup Sherry or Cognac or whiskey and enough of the broth from the liver to make a fine paste.

Line a casserole or loaf tin with slices of salt pork. Then put down a layer of the meat mixture. Imbed the peeled, hard-boiled eggs in the meat. Sprinkle with chopped green onions and parsley, add a little Cognac or whiskey, then cover with meat mixture. Next make a layer of thinly sliced pieces of pork, sprinkle with chopped green onions and parsley, add a little more Cognac or whiskey and some freshly ground black pepper. Cover again with the mixture and then salt pork slices. Bake covered for 2-1/2 hours at 325°. Take from the oven, remove cover and place a weight on the pâté to cool. When it is cool, remove the weight and store the pâté in refrigerator till ready to use. Slice very thin.

Serve with hot buttered toast, pumpernickel or hot French bread.

QUICK PÂTÉ

Combine 1 pound good liverwurst, 1/2 pound cream cheese, 1/2 cup raw mushrooms, chopped fine, 1 garlic clove crushed and chopped and 1/4 cup Cognac or whiskey. Beat well together, form into a loaf and serve with toast and buttered thin slices of bread.

BREAD AND SANDWICHES

HOT HERBED BREAD

Split loaves of French bread the long way. Spread with a mixture of 1/2 cup each chopped green onions, parsley butter with 1 teaspoon salt, 1 teaspoon freshly ground black pepper, and 1 tablespoon fresh or dried tarragon or 1 teaspoon thyme. Press the two pieces together and heat in a 400° oven for 10 to 15 minutes. Cut in 3–4 inch lengths. Serve piping hot with the butter melted well into the bread and the herbs heated through.

SESAME SEED BREAD

Split loaves of French bread in half the long way. Spread with garlic-flavored butter and sprinkle heavily with sesame seeds. Heat in a 400° oven for 10 minutes and brown under the broiler for 3–4 minutes. Cut in 3–4 inch chunks.

CHEESE AND HERB SANDWICH

Split loaves of French bread in halves the long way. Make a paste of 1/2 pound butter, 1/2 pound grated Switzerland Swiss cheese, 1/2 cup chopped green onions, 1/2 cup chopped parsley. Spread the halves with this mixture and press them together. Heat in a 400° oven for 12–15 minutes or until cheese and butter are melted.

HOT AND PUNGENT CHEESE SANDWICH

Combine 1/2 pound grated Switzerland Swiss cheese with 1 teaspoon dry mustard, 1 tablespoon curry powder, 1/2 cup chutney and blend well. Spread split loaves of French bread with the mixture and heat at 400° until the mixture is hot and bubbly and the bread crisp.

INDIVIDUAL HERO SANDWICHES

Split small crisp French rolls in halves the long way. Butter them well. On each roll place a few thin slices of tomato, salami, cheese, licked peppers, anchovies and sliced ripe olives. Press together and cut in halves. These are substantial and excellent for a large party.

THIN SANDWICHES

A well-made sandwich, of thin bread with plenty of butter and filling, is just about the most satisfying cocktail accompaniment.

Use good breads: pumpernickel, rye, thinly sliced white or whole-wheat bread, protein bread. Spread the slices well with unsalted butter and fill lavishly. Cut the crusts from the sandwiches and cut them into fingers—no fancy shapes are necessary. Pack them in foil and store them in the refrigerator for several hours before serving. Or freeze them the week before and thaw just before serving.

Here is a list of fillings that are very successful for cocktail service:

Thin slices of real Virginia ham
Good smoked ham with pungent mustard
Rare roast beef with horseradish butter
Turkey or white meat of chicken with mayonnaise
Thin slices of corned beef or pastrami
Chopped seeded and peeled tomato
Thin slices of cucumber
Thin slices of onion
Thin slices of onion with parsley and mayonnaise
Chopped ripe olives and onions with mayonnaise
Chopped shrimp with curry mayonnaise
Chopped chicken gizzards and hearts with chutney and fresh ginger
Chopped gizzards with mayonnaise and chopped green onion
Chopped chicken liver with egg and onion
Chopped anchovies, hard-boiled eggs, green onions, parsley
Chopped olives, pimentos, nuts, garlic parsley
Thin slices of salami
Thin slices of smoked salmon with cream cheese and onion
Thin slices of smoked sturgeon

Pâté de foie (tinned) on white bread with plenty of butter
Chopped cucumber, tomato, onion, ripe olive
Thin slices of tongue with hot mustard

SMOKED FISH

The pungence of smoked fish provokes thirst. It's a waste of time to cut up bits of fish and serve them on toast. Rather, serve a platter of various kinds with bread and butter, crackers, a little oil and vinegar, capers, a pepper mill and a pile of thinly sliced onions. Among my favorites are paper-thin slices of pink smoked salmon, marble-like slices of smoked sturgeon, whole smoked whitefish, smoked butterfish. Smoked eel is elegant. Smoked tuna and smoked cod are wonderful.

HERRING WITH SOUR CREAM

Chop 6 or 8 fillets of pickled herring rather coarsely—enough to make 2 cups. Combine with 1 cup each of mayonnaise and heavy sour cream. Season with 1/4 cup each chopped dill and chopped shallots or green onions. Provide a ladle and plenty of thin rye bread.

CANNED FISH

No matter where you are, you'll find canned smoked fish on the market. Thinly sliced smoked salmon is available, also smoked sturgeon, smoked cod, smoked shad, smoked tuna, salmon in a solid pack. Most come in various sizes. I recommend keeping a stock of canned fish on hand for those occasions when you want to offer a snack and drinks.

Sardines of various kinds, served in the can accompanied by toast and crackers, are another favorite cocktail standby.

FOOD FOR A LARGE PARTY

BAKED HAM

A large ham—Virginia, Tennessee or Georgia country ham —is delicious with cocktails. Serve a good-sized one, and be sure there's someone who knows how to carve it in thin, thin pieces across the top. Have bits of thinly cut small French bread and a selection of mustards. The flavor of ham helps to make cocktails more delectable, and there is no waste.

ROAST TURKEY

Turkey has the same good qualities that make a ham so pleasant with drinks. There is no waste and it is better to have some good turkey meat left over than a lot of spreads. Serve it with buttered bread and toast and some good pickles and relish and a bowl of raw vegetables and a good dip.

ROAST BEEF

A large roast of rare beef—just warm, not hot—and slabs of well-buttered and thinly sliced bread are unbeatable for a substantial cocktail snack. Be sure the carver slices the beef as thin as possible, and that you provide good mustard and horseradish with sour cream.

THE THING

This simple "thing" will be consumed by the quart. Children like it, and so do grandparents.

Combine various breakfast cereals: bit-size hunks, oatmeal cereal that comes in tiny rings, the crispies and crunchies that have body. To 2 quarts of the cereal add 1 pound small peanuts, a good sprinkling of Spice Islands garlic seasoning powder, a good sprinkling of chili powder. Salt to taste and dot well with butter. Toast at 300°–325° for 45 minutes to an hour. Shake the pan often and mix well with a spoon or fork so that there is an evenness of browning and crisping and mixing in of flavors. Salt and serve. Store in air-tight containers.

ON YOUR SHELVES

Here's a list of things you can keep on hand for times when you want to have a snack with a drink without too much bother:

Ripe olives or green olivcs; chill and serve or mix them with a little olive oil and garlic.

Stuffed olives

Cheese biscuits: there are some fabulous Dutch cheese crackers made like puff paste. Heat them and serve.

Anchovies in olive oil. Merely open a good-sized tin and serve with crackers or bread. Lemon should be around.

Sardines of all descriptions

Herring tidbits in tins

Smoked oysters

Tiny cocktail sausages

Tiny cocktail shrimp

Parched corn.

INDEX